Consider The Ant - God's Tiny Preachers

Joshua Rhoades

Published by Joshua Paul Rhoades, 2024.

While every precaution has been taken in the preparation of this book, the publisher assumes no responsibility for errors or omissions, or for damages resulting from the use of the information contained herein.

CONSIDER THE ANT - GOD'S TINY PREACHERS

First edition. August 22, 2024.

Copyright © 2024 Joshua Rhoades.

ISBN: 979-8227964335

Written by Joshua Rhoades.

Also by Joshua Rhoades

Courage Under Fire: David's Stand On The Battlefield

Jonah's Journey: Voices Of Redemption And Lessons In Obedience

The Furnace Of Faith: 12 Principles From The Heat Of Faith

Whispers of Hope: Inspiring Stories of Men's Prayers In Scripture

Frontier Legends: The Oregon Dream

Elijah: A Beacon Of Boldness

HOOK, LINE & SAVIOUR - Faith Reflections from Fishing

Driven By Faith: Motor Racing Inspired Christian Life

30 Day Devotional - Bold and Strong- Coffee Devotions for a
Courageous Christian Walk

Authentic Christianity: The Heart of Old Time Religion

Consider The Ant - God's Tiny Preachers

Flee Fornication: The Plea For Purity

Renewed Hope- How to Find Encouragement in God

Sounding The Call - The Voice of Conviction

The Altar - Where Heaven Meets Earth

The Sacred Art of Silence - How Silence Speaks in Scripture

Under Fire- The Sanctity of the Traditional Biblical Home

Who Is on the Lord's Side? A Call to Righteousness

Introduction

In the vast and intricate world of creation, God has embedded profound lessons within the smallest of creatures, urging us to look beyond the obvious and consider the wisdom of the ant. In "Consider The Ant - God's Tiny Preachers," we look into the remarkable world of ants, those tiny but powerful teachers, whose lives reflect spiritual truths that can profoundly impact our walk with God. Proverbs 6:6 beckons us to "Go to the ant, thou sluggard; consider her ways, and be wise:" a call to observe and emulate the diligence, unity, and perseverance exemplified by these seemingly insignificant insects. Each type of ant, from the tireless worker to the vigilant soldier, reveals a facet of the Christian life, offering us insights into how we can better serve, protect, and and lead. The worker ant, with its relentless dedication to gathering food and caring for the colony, mirrors the Christian's call to service, reminding us that no task in God's kingdom is too small or insignificant. The soldier ant, ever on guard to defend the colony, symbolizes the Christian's role in spiritual warfare, standing firm in the faith and safeguarding the truths of the gospel. Meanwhile, the queen ant, the heart of the colony, quietly embodies leadership and purpose, reflecting the importance of fulfilling our God-given roles with grace and dedication. Finally, the ant colony as a whole serves as a powerful metaphor for the local church, where each member, no matter how small, contributes to honoring the Lord, creating a thriving, harmonious body that mirrors the unity and effectiveness God desires for His church. As we explore these tiny preachers throughout this book, may we be inspired to embrace the lessons they offer, applying them to our lives so that we, too, may walk in wisdom, diligence, and unity, fulfilling our divine purpose in the grand design of God's kingdom.

Chapter 1 - Structuring Wood-Carpenter Ants

Proverbs 6:6 says, "Go to the ant, thou sluggard; consider her ways, and be wise." This verse encourages Christians to observe the diligent and structured behavior of ants, which parallels the Christian principle of building their lives on a solid foundation. Specifically, carpenter ants, known for structuring wood to build their nests, provide a powerful metaphor for Christians. Just as carpenter ants build their homes in wood, Christians are called to build their lives on the solid foundation of Jesus Christ. This foundational principle is crucial in a Christian's life, as it ensures stability, strength, and resilience in their spiritual journey.

Matthew 7:24-25 says, "Therefore whosoever heareth these sayings of mine, and doeth them, I will liken him unto a wise man, which built his house upon a rock: And the rain descended, and the floods came, and the winds blew, and beat upon that house; and it fell not: for it was founded upon a rock." This verse highlights the importance of hearing and obeying Jesus' teachings, likening it to a wise man who builds his house on a rock. Just as carpenter ants meticulously structure their nests in wood for stability, Christians are called to build their lives on the unshakable foundation of Christ's words. When life's storms come, those who have built their lives on this solid foundation will remain steadfast and secure.

1 Corinthians 3:10-11 teaches, "According to the grace of God which is given unto me, as a wise masterbuilder, I have laid the foundation, and another buildeth thereon. But let every man take heed how he buildeth thereupon. For other foundation can no man lay than that is laid, which is Jesus Christ." This passage emphasizes that Jesus Christ is the only true foundation upon which Christians should build their lives. Just as carpenter ants choose sturdy wood for their nests, believers must ensure that their lives are anchored in Christ. By doing

so, they can build upon this foundation with faith, love, and obedience, creating a life that honors God and withstands the tests of time.

Applying these principles to our lives means developing a mindset of constructing our spiritual lives on the teachings and example of Jesus Christ. In our daily devotions, this means setting aside regular time for prayer, Bible study, and worship, making these activities a priority despite the busyness of life. Just as carpenter ants are consistent in their work of building, Christians should be consistent in their spiritual practices, knowing that these disciplines strengthen their relationship with God and help them grow in faith.

In our thoughts and attitudes, structuring our lives on the foundation of Christ involves setting clear priorities and avoiding distractions that hinder our spiritual growth. This means focusing on God's promises and truths rather than being swayed by worldly concerns or negative influences. By keeping our thoughts centered on God and organizing our activities around His will, we can maintain a positive and faith-filled perspective, even in challenging circumstances.

In our actions, building on the foundation of Christ involves living out our faith with intentionality and purpose. This means making deliberate choices that honor God and reflect His character, whether in our work, relationships, or daily interactions. Just as carpenter ants work diligently to create a stable and secure nest, Christians are called to act in ways that build up the body of Christ and serve others. By staying focused on God's mission for our lives, we can make a meaningful impact in the world and advance His kingdom.

In our relationships, building on the foundation of Christ means being intentional about building and maintaining connections that encourage spiritual growth and mutual support. Just as carpenter ants work together to strengthen their nest, Christians are called to live in unity and support one another in their faith journeys. This involves being present for each other, offering encouragement and

accountability, and prioritizing relationships that draw us closer to God.

In our use of time and resources, building on the foundation of Christ involves being good stewards of what God has given us, using our time, talents, and treasures for His glory. Just as carpenter ants manage their resources efficiently, Christians should use their gifts and abilities to serve God and others, making the most of every opportunity to do good. This includes setting goals, managing our time wisely, and being generous with our resources.

The example of carpenter ants also teaches us about the importance of perseverance and resilience in building on the foundation of Christ. Carpenter ants do not give up when faced with obstacles but continue to work diligently until their nests are secure. Similarly, Christians are called to persevere in their faith, even when faced with trials and difficulties. James 1:12 encourages, "Blessed is the man that endureth temptation: for when he is tried, he shall receive the crown of life, which the Lord hath promised to them that love him." By persevering in building their lives on Christ, believers can grow in their faith and receive the blessings God has promised.

In addition to practical applications, building on the foundation of Christ has deep spiritual significance. Jesus demonstrated the ultimate example of building a life on God's will during His time on earth. In John 17:4, Jesus said, "I have glorified thee on the earth: I have finished the work which thou gavest me to do." Jesus was completely focused on fulfilling God's will and remained faithful to His mission until the end. His single-minded dedication to His mission serves as a powerful example for Christians to follow. By developing a mindset of building their lives on the foundation of Christ, believers can emulate Christ's example and grow in their likeness to Him.

Building on the foundation of Christ also plays a crucial role in spiritual growth and maturity. By staying focused on God's purposes and using our gifts to serve others, Christians can avoid the distractions and temptations that hinder their spiritual growth. Hebrews 12:1-2 encourages believers to "lay aside every weight, and the sin which doth so easily beset us, and let us run with patience the race that is set before us, Looking unto Jesus the author and finisher of our faith." This verse emphasizes the importance of removing distractions and focusing on Jesus as we pursue our spiritual goals. By maintaining a mindset of building on Christ, believers can grow in their faith and become more effective in their service to God and others.

The principle of building on the foundation of Christ also teaches us about the importance of integrity and consistency. Just as carpenter ants are consistent in their work, Christians are called to live with integrity and consistency in their faith. This means being the same person in private as we are in public, and living out our faith in all areas of life. By maintaining a mindset of building on Christ, believers can build a strong and authentic witness that draws others to Him.

Building on the foundation of Christ also involves setting priorities and making intentional choices. Just as carpenter ants prioritize their tasks for the stability of their nest, Christians should prioritize their activities to align with God's purposes. This involves seeking God's guidance in decision-making, setting goals that reflect His will, and being intentional about how we spend our time and energy. By prioritizing God's kingdom and righteousness, believers can ensure that their efforts are focused on what truly matters.

In conclusion, Proverbs 6:6 teaches Christians to observe the carpenter ant and learn from its diligent and structured behavior. The example of carpenter ants structuring wood to build their nests illustrates the Christian principle of building their lives on the solid foundation of Jesus Christ. By applying these principles to our lives, we can develop a mindset of building on Christ, achieve our goals, and grow in our relationship with God. Whether it is in our daily devotions, thoughts, actions, relationships, or use of time and resources, we are called to maintain a mindset of building on the foundation of Christ. This not only brings us personal fulfillment but also glorifies God and reflects His love and wisdom to those around us. Through diligent construction of our lives on Jesus, we can overcome challenges, grow stronger in our faith, and make a positive impact in the world.

Chapter 2 – Stinging - Fire Ants

Proverbs 6:6 says, "Go to the ant, thou sluggard; consider her ways, and be wise." This verse encourages Christians to learn from the diligent and strategic behavior of ants, which parallels the Christian principle of vigilance and protection against spiritual attacks. Fire ants, known for their defensive nature and powerful stings, provide a potent metaphor for Christians. Just as fire ants are vigilant in defending their colony, Christians are called to be vigilant and protect their faith against spiritual attacks. This defensive stance is crucial in a Christian's life, as it ensures the preservation and strengthening of their faith in the face of adversities.

Ephesians 6:11 says, "Put on the whole armour of God, that ye may be able to stand against the wiles of the devil." This verse highlights the importance of being fully equipped with God's armor to withstand the schemes of the devil. Just as fire ants use their stings to defend their colony, Christians are called to put on the armor of God, which includes the belt of truth, the breastplate of righteousness, the shield of faith, the helmet of salvation, and the sword of the Spirit. This spiritual armor enables believers to stand firm against the devil's attacks and protect their faith effectively.

1 Peter 5:8 teaches, "Be sober, be vigilant; because your adversary the devil, as a roaring lion, walketh about, seeking whom he may devour." This verse emphasizes the need for vigilance and alertness. Just as fire ants are constantly on guard to protect their colony, Christians must be vigilant and aware of the devil's attempts to devour their faith. Being sober and vigilant means staying spiritually alert, resisting temptation, and being prepared to defend one's faith against any form of spiritual attack.

Applying these principles to our lives means developing a mindset of vigilance and protection in various aspects of our spiritual journey. In our daily devotions, this means setting aside regular time for prayer, Bible study, and worship, making these activities a priority despite the busyness of life. Just as fire ants are consistent in their defense, Christians should be consistent in their spiritual practices, knowing that these disciplines strengthen their relationship with God and help them grow in faith.

In our thoughts and attitudes, vigilance and protection involve setting clear priorities and avoiding distractions that hinder our spiritual growth. This means focusing on God's promises and truths rather than being swayed by worldly concerns or negative influences. By keeping our thoughts centered on God and organizing our activities around His will, we can maintain a positive and faith-filled perspective, even in challenging circumstances.

In our actions, vigilance and protection involve living out our faith with intentionality and purpose. This means making deliberate choices that honor God and reflect His character, whether in our work, relationships, or daily interactions. Just as fire ants work diligently to protect their colony, Christians are called to act in ways that build up the body of Christ and serve others. By staying focused on God's mission for our lives, we can make a meaningful impact in the world and advance His kingdom.

In our relationships, vigilance and protection mean being intentional about building and maintaining connections that encourage spiritual growth and mutual support. Just as fire ants work together to defend their colony, Christians are called to live in unity and support one another in their faith journeys. This involves being present for each other, offering encouragement and accountability, and prioritizing relationships that draw us closer to God.

In our use of time and resources, vigilance and protection involve being good stewards of what God has given us, using our time, talents, and treasures for His glory. Just as fire ants manage their resources efficiently, Christians should use their gifts and abilities to serve God and others, making the most of every opportunity to do good. This includes setting goals, managing our time wisely, and being generous with our resources.

The example of fire ants also teaches us about the importance of perseverance and resilience in maintaining vigilance and protection. Fire ants do not give up when faced with threats but continue to defend their colony until the danger is eliminated. Similarly, Christians are called to persevere in their faith, even when faced with trials and difficulties. James 1:12 encourages, "Blessed is the man that endureth temptation: for when he is tried, he shall receive the crown of life, which the Lord hath promised to them that love him." By persevering in vigilance and protection, believers can grow in their faith and receive the blessings God has promised.

In addition to practical applications, vigilance and protection have deep spiritual significance. Jesus demonstrated the ultimate example of vigilance during His time on earth. In Matthew 26:41, Jesus said, "Watch and pray, that ye enter not into temptation: the spirit indeed is willing, but the flesh is weak." Jesus was completely focused on fulfilling God's will and remained vigilant in prayer and obedience. His single-minded dedication to His mission serves as a powerful example for Christians to follow. By developing a mindset of vigilance and protection, believers can emulate Christ's example and grow in their likeness to Him.

Vigilance and protection also play a crucial role in spiritual growth and maturity. By staying focused on God's purposes and using our gifts to serve others, Christians can avoid the distractions and temptations that hinder their spiritual growth. Hebrews 12:1-2 encourages believers to "lay aside every weight, and the sin which doth so easily beset us, and let us run with patience the race that is set before us, Looking unto Jesus the author and finisher of our faith." This verse emphasizes the importance of removing distractions and focusing on Jesus as we pursue our spiritual goals. By maintaining a mindset of vigilance and protection, believers can grow in their faith and become more effective in their service to God and others.

The principle of vigilance and protection also teaches us about the importance of integrity and consistency. Just as fire ants are consistent in their defense, Christians are called to live with integrity and consistency in their faith. This means being the same person in private as we are in public, and living out our faith in all areas of life. By maintaining a mindset of vigilance and protection, believers can build a strong and authentic witness that draws others to Christ.

Vigilance and protection also involve setting priorities and making intentional choices. Just as fire ants prioritize the defense of their colony, Christians should prioritize their activities to align with God's purposes. This involves seeking God's guidance in decision-making, setting goals that reflect His will, and being intentional about how we spend our time and energy. By prioritizing God's kingdom and righteousness, believers can ensure that their efforts are focused on what truly matters.

In conclusion, Proverbs 6:6 teaches Christians to observe the fire ant and learn from its vigilant and defensive behavior. The example of fire ants defending their colony illustrates the Christian principle of being vigilant and protecting their faith against spiritual attacks. By applying these principles to our lives, we can develop a mindset of vigilance and protection, achieve our goals, and grow in our relationship with God. Whether it is in our daily devotions, thoughts, actions, relationships, or use of time and resources, we are called to maintain a mindset of vigilance and protection. This not only brings us personal fulfillment but also glorifies God and reflects His love and wisdom to those around us. Through vigilant defense of our faith, we can overcome challenges, grow stronger in our faith, and make a positive impact in the world.

Chapater 3 – Sourcing Leaves - Leafcutter Ants

Proverbs 6:6 says, "Go to the ant, thou sluggard; consider her ways, and be wise." This verse encourages Christians to learn from the diligent and resourceful behavior of ants, which parallels the Christian principle of diligently seeking God's Word for spiritual nourishment. Leafcutter ants, known for their tireless efforts in sourcing leaves to cultivate their fungus gardens, provide a vivid metaphor for Christians. Just as leafcutter ants diligently gather leaves to sustain their colony, Christians are called to diligently seek and study God's Word to nourish their spiritual lives. This diligent pursuit is crucial in a Christian's life, as it ensures growth, strength, and resilience in their walk with the Lord.

Proverbs 12:27 says, "The slothful man roasteth not that which he took in hunting: but the substance of a diligent man is precious." This verse highlights the value of diligence over laziness. Just as leafcutter ants work tirelessly to gather leaves for their fungus gardens, Christians should be diligent in their study of the Bible. The substance of a diligent man's efforts is precious, reflecting the deep spiritual nourishment and wisdom that comes from earnestly seeking and applying God's Word. By being diligent, Christians can avoid the pitfalls of spiritual laziness and reap the precious rewards of a close, fulfilling relationship with God.

2 Timothy 2:15 teaches, "Study to shew thyself approved unto God, a workman that needeth not to be ashamed, rightly dividing the word of truth." This verse emphasizes the importance of studying the Scriptures diligently. Just as leafcutter ants meticulously gather leaves to sustain their colony, Christians are called to study God's Word with dedication and precision. By rightly dividing the word of truth, believers can gain a deeper understanding of God's will and live lives

that are pleasing to Him. This diligent study equips Christians to handle the Word accurately and apply it effectively in their daily lives.

Applying these principles to our lives means developing a mindset of diligence in seeking spiritual nourishment in various aspects of our spiritual journey. In our daily devotions, this means setting aside regular time for prayer, Bible study, and worship, making these activities a priority despite the busyness of life. Just as leafcutter ants are consistent in their gathering of leaves, Christians should be consistent in their spiritual practices, knowing that these disciplines strengthen their relationship with God and help them grow in faith.

In our thoughts and attitudes, seeking spiritual nourishment involves setting clear priorities and avoiding distractions that hinder our spiritual growth. This means focusing on God's promises and truths rather than being swayed by worldly concerns or negative influences. By keeping our thoughts centered on God and organizing our activities around His will, we can maintain a positive and faith-filled perspective, even in challenging circumstances.

In our actions, diligently seeking God's Word involves living out our faith with intentionality and purpose. This means making deliberate choices that honor God and reflect His character, whether in our work, relationships, or daily interactions. Just as leafcutter ants work diligently for the good of their colony, Christians are called to act in ways that build up the body of Christ and serve others. By staying focused on God's mission for our lives, we can make a meaningful impact in the world and advance His kingdom.

In our relationships, diligently seeking spiritual nourishment means being intentional about building and maintaining connections that encourage spiritual growth and mutual support. Just as leafcutter ants work together for the benefit of the colony, Christians are called to live in unity and support one another in their faith journeys. This involves being present for each other, offering encouragement and

accountability, and prioritizing relationships that draw us closer to God.

In our use of time and resources, diligently seeking spiritual nourishment involves being good stewards of what God has given us, using our time, talents, and treasures for His glory. Just as leafcutter ants manage their resources efficiently, Christians should use their gifts and abilities to serve God and others, making the most of every opportunity to do good. This includes setting goals, managing our time wisely, and being generous with our resources.

The example of leafcutter ants also teaches us about the importance of perseverance and resilience in seeking spiritual nourishment. Leafcutter ants do not give up when faced with obstacles but continue to work diligently until their tasks are complete. Similarly, Christians are called to persevere in their faith, even when faced with trials and difficulties. James 1:12 encourages, "Blessed is the man that endureth temptation: for when he is tried, he shall receive the crown of life, which the Lord hath promised to them that love him." By persevering in seeking God's Word, believers can grow in their faith and receive the blessings God has promised.

In addition to practical applications, diligently seeking spiritual nourishment has deep spiritual significance. Jesus demonstrated the ultimate example of seeking God's Word during His time on earth. In John 5:39, Jesus said, "Search the scriptures; for in them ye think ye have eternal life: and they are they which testify of me." Jesus was completely focused on fulfilling God's will and remained diligent in His study and application of the Scriptures. His single-minded dedication to His mission serves as a powerful example for Christians to follow. By developing a mindset of diligently seeking God's Word, believers can emulate Christ's example and grow in their likeness to Him.

Diligently seeking spiritual nourishment also plays a crucial role in spiritual growth and maturity. By staying focused on God's purposes and using our gifts to serve others, Christians can avoid the distractions and temptations that hinder their spiritual growth. Hebrews 12:1-2 encourages believers to "lay aside every weight, and the sin which doth so easily beset us, and let us run with patience the race that is set before us, Looking unto Jesus the author and finisher of our faith." This verse emphasizes the importance of removing distractions and focusing on Jesus as we pursue our spiritual goals. By maintaining a mindset of diligently seeking God's Word, believers can grow in their faith and become more effective in their service to God and others.

The principle of diligently seeking spiritual nourishment also teaches us about the importance of integrity and consistency. Just as leafcutter ants are consistent in their work, Christians are called to live with integrity and consistency in their faith. This means being the same person in private as we are in public, and living out our faith in all areas of life. By maintaining a mindset of diligently seeking God's Word, believers can build a strong and authentic witness that draws others to Christ.

Diligently seeking spiritual nourishment also involves setting priorities and making intentional choices. Just as leafcutter ants prioritize their tasks for the benefit of their colony, Christians should prioritize their activities to align with God's purposes. This involves seeking God's guidance in decision-making, setting goals that reflect His will, and being intentional about how we spend our time and energy. By prioritizing God's kingdom and righteousness, believers can ensure that their efforts are focused on what truly matters.

In conclusion, Proverbs 6:6 teaches Christians to observe the leafcutter ant and learn from its diligent and resourceful behavior. The example of leafcutter ants sourcing leaves for their fungus gardens illustrates the Christian principle of diligently seeking God's Word for spiritual nourishment. By applying these principles to our lives, we can develop a mindset of diligence in seeking God's Word, achieve our goals, and grow in our relationship with God. Whether it is in our daily devotions, thoughts, actions, relationships, or use of time and resources, we are called to maintain a mindset of diligently seeking spiritual nourishment. This not only brings us personal fulfillment but also glorifies God and reflects His love and wisdom to those around us. Through diligent study and application of God's Word, we can overcome challenges, grow stronger in our faith, and make a positive impact in the world.

Chapter 4 – Silk-Weaving - Weaver Ants

Proverbs 6:6 says, "Go to the ant, thou sluggard; consider her ways, and be wise." This verse encourages Christians to learn from the diligent and cooperative behavior of ants, which parallels the Christian principle of unity and teamwork within the community. Weaver ants, known for their intricate silk-weaving to construct complex nests, provide a vivid metaphor for Christians. Just as weaver ants collaborate to create strong and secure nests, Christians are called to work together in unity to build up the body of Christ. This cooperative spirit is crucial in a Christian's life, as it fosters harmony, strength, and mutual support within the faith community.

Ephesians 4:3 says, "Endeavouring to keep the unity of the Spirit in the bond of peace." This verse highlights the importance of striving for unity in the Spirit and maintaining peace among believers. Just as weaver ants work tirelessly and harmoniously to build their nests, Christians are called to make every effort to keep the unity of the Spirit through the bond of peace. This involves setting aside personal differences and working together for the common good, reflecting the love and unity that Christ desires for His followers.

Colossians 3:14 teaches, "And above all these things put on charity, which is the bond of perfectness." This verse emphasizes the supreme importance of love in binding believers together in perfect unity. Just as weaver ants use silk to bind leaves and construct their nests, Christians are called to put on love, which holds everything together in perfect harmony. Love is the glue that binds the Christian community, enabling believers to support and uplift one another.

Applying these principles to our lives means developing a mindset of unity and teamwork in various aspects of our spiritual journey. In our daily devotions, this means setting aside regular time for prayer, Bible study, and worship, making these activities a priority despite the busyness of life. Just as weaver ants are consistent in their collaborative efforts, Christians should be consistent in their spiritual practices, knowing that these disciplines strengthen their relationship with God and help them grow in faith.

In our thoughts and attitudes, unity and teamwork involve setting clear priorities and avoiding distractions that hinder our spiritual growth. This means focusing on God's promises and truths rather than being swayed by worldly concerns or negative influences. By keeping our thoughts centered on God and organizing our activities around His will, we can maintain a positive and faith-filled perspective, even in challenging circumstances.

In our actions, unity and teamwork involve living out our faith with intentionality and purpose. This means making deliberate choices that honor God and reflect His character, whether in our work, relationships, or daily interactions. Just as weaver ants work diligently for the good of their colony, Christians are called to act in ways that build up the body of Christ and serve others. By staying focused on God's mission for our lives, we can make a meaningful impact in the world and advance His kingdom.

In our relationships, unity and teamwork mean being intentional about building and maintaining connections that encourage spiritual growth and mutual support. Just as weaver ants work together to construct their nests, Christians are called to live in unity and support one another in their faith journeys. This involves being present for each other, offering encouragement and accountability, and prioritizing relationships that draw us closer to God.

In our use of time and resources, unity and teamwork involve being good stewards of what God has given us, using our time, talents, and treasures for His glory. Just as weaver ants manage their resources efficiently, Christians should use their gifts and abilities to serve God and others, making the most of every opportunity to do good. This includes setting goals, managing our time wisely, and being generous with our resources.

The example of weaver ants also teaches us about the importance of perseverance and resilience in maintaining unity and teamwork. Weaver ants do not give up when faced with obstacles but continue to work diligently until their nests are secure. Similarly, Christians are called to persevere in their faith, even when faced with trials and difficulties. James 1:12 encourages, "Blessed is the man that endureth temptation: for when he is tried, he shall receive the crown of life, which the Lord hath promised to them that love him." By persevering in unity and teamwork, believers can grow in their faith and receive the blessings God has promised.

In addition to practical applications, unity and teamwork have deep spiritual significance. Jesus demonstrated the ultimate example of unity and teamwork during His time on earth. In John 17:21, Jesus prayed, "That they all may be one; as thou, Father, art in me, and I in thee, that they also may be one in us: that the world may believe that thou hast sent me." Jesus was completely focused on fulfilling God's will and desired unity among His followers. His single-minded dedication to His mission serves as a powerful example for Christians to follow. By developing a mindset of unity and teamwork, believers can emulate Christ's example and grow in their likeness to Him.

Unity and teamwork also play a crucial role in spiritual growth and maturity. By staying focused on God's purposes and using our gifts to serve others, Christians can avoid the distractions and temptations that hinder their spiritual growth. Hebrews 12:1-2 encourages believers to "lay aside every weight, and the sin which doth so easily beset us, and let us run with patience the race that is set before us, Looking unto Jesus the author and finisher of our faith." This verse emphasizes the importance of removing distractions and focusing on Jesus as we pursue our spiritual goals. By maintaining a mindset of unity and teamwork, believers can grow in their faith and become more effective in their service to God and others.

The principle of unity and teamwork also teaches us about the importance of integrity and consistency. Just as weaver ants are consistent in their collaborative efforts, Christians are called to live with integrity and consistency in their faith. This means being the same person in private as we are in public, and living out our faith in all areas of life. By maintaining a mindset of unity and teamwork, believers can build a strong and authentic witness that draws others to Christ.

Unity and teamwork also involve setting priorities and making intentional choices. Just as weaver ants prioritize their tasks for the stability of their nest, Christians should prioritize their activities to align with God's purposes. This involves seeking God's guidance in decision-making, setting goals that reflect His will, and being intentional about how we spend our time and energy. By prioritizing God's kingdom and righteousness, believers can ensure that their efforts are focused on what truly matters.

In conclusion, Proverbs 6:6 teaches Christians to observe the weaver ant and learn from its diligent and cooperative behavior. The example of weaver ants constructing complex nests through cooperation illustrates the Christian principle of unity and teamwork within the community. By applying these principles to our lives, we can develop a mindset of unity and teamwork, achieve our goals, and grow in our relationship with God. Whether it is in our daily devotions, thoughts, actions, relationships, or use of time and resources, we are called to maintain a mindset of unity and teamwork. This not only brings us personal fulfillment but also glorifies God and reflects His love and wisdom to those around us. Through cooperative efforts and dedication, we can overcome challenges, grow stronger in our faith, and make a positive impact in the world.

Chapter 5 - Swarming - Army Ants

Proverbs 6:6 says, "Go to the ant, thou sluggard; consider her ways, and be wise." This verse encourages Christians to learn from the diligent and coordinated behavior of ants, which parallels the Christian principle of unity and teamwork in spreading the gospel. Army ants, known for their coordinated swarming behavior, provide a vivid metaphor for Christians. Just as army ants move and act together in a unified manner, Christians are called to work together as a unified body to spread the gospel. This coordinated effort is crucial in a Christian's life, as it fosters strength, effectiveness, and unity in fulfilling the Great Commission.

1 Corinthians 12:12 says, "For as the body is one, and hath many members, and all the members of that one body, being many, are one body: so also is Christ." This verse highlights the importance of unity within the body of Christ. Just as army ants operate as a single, coordinated unit, Christians are called to function as one body, despite being many members. Each member has a unique role, but together they form a cohesive whole that is capable of accomplishing great things for God's kingdom. This unity is essential for the effective spread of the gospel and the building up of the church.

Philippians 1:27 teaches, "Only let your conversation be as it becometh the gospel of Christ: that whether I come and see you, or else be absent, I may hear of your affairs, that ye stand fast in one spirit, with one mind striving together for the faith of the gospel." This verse emphasizes the need for Christians to stand firm in one spirit and strive together with one mind for the faith of the gospel. Just as army ants work together with a common purpose, Christians are called to be unified in their efforts to spread the gospel. This involves setting aside personal differences and working together for the common goal of advancing God's kingdom.

Applying these principles to our lives means developing a mindset of unity and coordination in various aspects of our spiritual journey. In our daily devotions, this means setting aside regular time for prayer, Bible study, and worship, making these activities a priority despite the busyness of life. Just as army ants are consistent in their coordinated efforts, Christians should be consistent in their spiritual practices, knowing that these disciplines strengthen their relationship with God and help them grow in faith.

In our thoughts and attitudes, unity and coordination involve setting clear priorities and avoiding distractions that hinder our spiritual growth. This means focusing on God's promises and truths rather than being swayed by worldly concerns or negative influences. By keeping our thoughts centered on God and organizing our activities around His will, we can maintain a positive and faith-filled perspective, even in challenging circumstances.

In our actions, unity and coordination involve living out our faith with intentionality and purpose. This means making deliberate choices that honor God and reflect His character, whether in our work, relationships, or daily interactions. Just as army ants work diligently for the good of their colony, Christians are called to act in ways that build up the body of Christ and serve others. By staying focused on God's mission for our lives, we can make a meaningful impact in the world and advance His kingdom.

In our relationships, unity and coordination mean being intentional about building and maintaining connections that encourage spiritual growth and mutual support. Just as army ants work together to achieve their goals, Christians are called to live in unity and support one another in their faith journeys. This involves being present for each other, offering encouragement and accountability, and prioritizing relationships that draw us closer to God.

In our use of time and resources, unity and coordination involve being good stewards of what God has given us, using our time, talents, and treasures for His glory. Just as army ants manage their resources efficiently, Christians should use their gifts and abilities to serve God and others, making the most of every opportunity to do good. This includes setting goals, managing our time wisely, and being generous with our resources.

The example of army ants also teaches us about the importance of perseverance and resilience in maintaining unity and coordination. Army ants do not give up when faced with obstacles but continue to work diligently until their tasks are complete. Similarly, Christians are called to persevere in their faith, even when faced with trials and difficulties. James 1:12 encourages, "Blessed is the man that endureth temptation: for when he is tried, he shall receive the crown of life, which the Lord hath promised to them that love him." By persevering in unity and coordination, believers can grow in their faith and receive the blessings God has promised.

In addition to practical applications, unity and coordination have deep spiritual significance. Jesus demonstrated the ultimate example of unity and coordination during His time on earth. In John 17:21, Jesus prayed, "That they all may be one; as thou, Father, art in me, and I in thee, that they also may be one in us: that the world may believe that thou hast sent me." Jesus was completely focused on fulfilling God's will and desired unity among His followers. His single-minded dedication to His mission serves as a powerful example for Christians to follow. By developing a mindset of unity and coordination, believers can emulate Christ's example and grow in their likeness to Him.

Unity and coordination also play a crucial role in spiritual growth and maturity. By staying focused on God's purposes and using our gifts to serve others, Christians can avoid the distractions and temptations that hinder their spiritual growth. Hebrews 12:1-2 encourages believers to "lay aside every weight, and the sin which doth so easily beset us, and let us run with patience the race that is set before us, Looking unto Jesus the author and finisher of our faith." This verse emphasizes the importance of removing distractions and focusing on Jesus as we pursue our spiritual goals. By maintaining a mindset of unity and coordination, believers can grow in their faith and become more effective in their service to God and others.

The principle of unity and coordination also teaches us about the importance of integrity and consistency. Just as army ants are consistent in their coordinated efforts, Christians are called to live with integrity and consistency in their faith. This means being the same person in private as we are in public, and living out our faith in all areas of life. By maintaining a mindset of unity and coordination, believers can build a strong and authentic witness that draws others to Christ.

Unity and coordination also involve setting priorities and making intentional choices. Just as army ants prioritize their tasks for the benefit of their colony, Christians should prioritize their activities to align with God's purposes. This involves seeking God's guidance in decision-making, setting goals that reflect His will, and being intentional about how we spend our time and energy. By prioritizing God's kingdom and righteousness, believers can ensure that their efforts are focused on what truly matters.

In conclusion, Proverbs 6:6 teaches Christians to observe the army ant and learn from its diligent and coordinated behavior. The example of army ants swarming together illustrates the Christian principle of moving and acting together as a unified body in spreading the gospel. By applying these principles to our lives, we can develop a mindset of unity and coordination, achieve our goals, and grow in our relationship with God. Whether it is in our daily devotions, thoughts, actions, relationships, or use of time and resources, we are called to maintain a mindset of unity and coordination. This not only brings us personal fulfillment but also glorifies God and reflects His love and wisdom to those around us. Through coordinated efforts and dedication, we can overcome challenges, grow stronger in our faith, and make a positive impact in the world.

Chapter 6 – Scenting - Odorous House Ants

Proverbs 6:6 says, "Go to the ant, thou sluggard; consider her ways, and be wise." This verse encourages Christians to learn from the behavior of ants, which parallels the Christian principle of being a pleasing aroma of Christ to others. Odorous house ants, known for releasing a distinct scent when crushed, provide a vivid metaphor for Christians. Just as these ants emit a noticeable fragrance, Christians are called to be a sweet aroma of Christ to those around them. This means living a life that reflects Christ's love and sacrifice, influencing others positively through their words and actions.

2 Corinthians 2:15 says, "For we are unto God a sweet savour of Christ, in them that are saved, and in them that perish." This verse highlights that Christians are a sweet fragrance of Christ to God among those who are being saved and those who are perishing. Just as the scent of odorous house ants is distinct and unmistakable, Christians should have a presence that unmistakably reflects Christ. Our lives should emit the fragrance of Christ's love, grace, and truth, impacting everyone we encounter, whether they accept or reject the gospel. This sweet savour is a testimony to God's work in us and through us.

Ephesians 5:2 teaches, "And walk in love, as Christ also hath loved us, and hath given himself for us an offering and a sacrifice to God for a sweet-smelling savour." This verse emphasizes the importance of walking in love, just as Christ loved us and gave Himself up for us as a fragrant offering and sacrifice to God. Just as odorous house ants release their scent as a natural response, Christians should naturally exude love, kindness, and compassion in all they do. By living a life of sacrificial love, believers can be a pleasing aroma to God and an attractive witness to others, drawing them to Christ.

Applying these principles to our lives means developing a mindset of being a sweet aroma of Christ in various aspects of our spiritual journey. In our daily devotions, this means setting aside regular time for prayer, Bible study, and worship, making these activities a priority despite the busyness of life. Just as odorous house ants consistently release their scent, Christians should consistently cultivate their relationship with God, knowing that these disciplines strengthen their relationship with Him and help them grow in faith.

In our thoughts and attitudes, being a sweet aroma involves setting clear priorities and avoiding distractions that hinder our spiritual growth. This means focusing on God's promises and truths rather than being swayed by worldly concerns or negative influences. By keeping our thoughts centered on God and organizing our activities around His will, we can maintain a positive and faith-filled perspective, even in challenging circumstances.

In our actions, being a sweet aroma of Christ involves living out our faith with intentionality and purpose. This means making deliberate choices that honor God and reflect His character, whether in our work, relationships, or daily interactions. Just as odorous house ants leave a lasting impression with their scent, Christians are called to leave a positive and lasting impact on those around them. By staying focused on God's mission for our lives, we can make a meaningful impact in the world and advance His kingdom.

In our relationships, being a sweet aroma means being intentional about building and maintaining connections that encourage spiritual growth and mutual support. Just as odorous house ants communicate through their scent, Christians are called to communicate God's love and grace through their actions and words. This involves being present for each other, offering encouragement and accountability, and prioritizing relationships that draw us closer to God.

In our use of time and resources, being a sweet aroma involves being good stewards of what God has given us, using our time, talents, and treasures for His glory. Just as odorous house ants manage their resources efficiently, Christians should use their gifts and abilities to serve God and others, making the most of every opportunity to do good. This includes setting goals, managing our time wisely, and being generous with our resources.

The example of odorous house ants also teaches us about the importance of perseverance and resilience in maintaining a pleasing aroma of Christ. Odorous house ants do not give up when faced with obstacles but continue to work diligently until their tasks are complete. Similarly, Christians are called to persevere in their faith, even when faced with trials and difficulties. James 1:12 encourages, "Blessed is the man that endureth temptation: for when he is tried, he shall receive the crown of life, which the Lord hath promised to them that love him." By persevering in being a sweet aroma of Christ, believers can grow in their faith and receive the blessings God has promised.

In addition to practical applications, being a sweet aroma of Christ has deep spiritual significance. Jesus demonstrated the ultimate example of being a sweet aroma during His time on earth. In John 13:34-35, Jesus said, "A new commandment I give unto you, That ye love one another; as I have loved you, that ye also love one another. By this shall all men know that ye are my disciples, if ye have love one to another." Jesus was completely focused on fulfilling God's will and remained diligent in His love and service to others. His single-minded dedication to His mission serves as a powerful example for Christians to follow. By developing a mindset of being a sweet aroma of Christ, believers can emulate Christ's example and grow in their likeness to Him.

Being a sweet aroma of Christ also plays a crucial role in spiritual growth and maturity. By staying focused on God's purposes and using our gifts to serve others, Christians can avoid the distractions and temptations that hinder their spiritual growth. Hebrews 12:1-2 encourages believers to "lay aside every weight, and the sin which doth so easily beset us, and let us run with patience the race that is set before us, Looking unto Jesus the author and finisher of our faith." This verse emphasizes the importance of removing distractions and focusing on Jesus as we pursue our spiritual goals. By maintaining a mindset of being a sweet aroma of Christ, believers can grow in their faith and become more effective in their service to God and others.

The principle of being a sweet aroma of Christ also teaches us about the importance of integrity and consistency. Just as odorous house ants are consistent in their scent, Christians are called to live with integrity and consistency in their faith. This means being the same person in private as we are in public, and living out our faith in all areas of life. By maintaining a mindset of being a sweet aroma of Christ, believers can build a strong and authentic witness that draws others to Him.

Being a sweet aroma of Christ also involves setting priorities and making intentional choices. Just as odorous house ants prioritize their tasks for the benefit of their colony, Christians should prioritize their activities to align with God's purposes. This involves seeking God's guidance in decision-making, setting goals that reflect His will, and being intentional about how we spend our time and energy. By prioritizing God's kingdom and righteousness, believers can ensure that their efforts are focused on what truly matters.

In conclusion, Proverbs 6:6 teaches Christians to observe the odorous house ant and learn from its distinctive behavior. The example of odorous house ants releasing a distinct scent illustrates the Christian principle of being a pleasing aroma of Christ to others. By applying these principles to our lives, we can develop a mindset of being a sweet aroma of Christ, achieve our goals, and grow in our relationship with God. Whether it is in our daily devotions, thoughts, actions, relationships, or use of time and resources, we are called to maintain a mindset of being a sweet aroma of Christ. This not only brings us personal fulfillment but also glorifies God and reflects His love and wisdom to those around us. Through living a life that is a pleasing aroma to God and others, we can overcome challenges, grow stronger in our faith, and make a positive impact in the world.

Chapter 7 – Scouting Indoors - Pharaoh Ants

Proverbs 6:6 says, "Go to the ant, thou sluggard; consider her ways, and be wise." This verse encourages Christians to observe the diligent and purposeful behavior of ants, which parallels the Christian principle of seeking out and sharing spiritual nourishment within their communities. Pharaoh ants, known for their ability to find food sources indoors, provide a vivid metaphor for Christians. Just as these ants meticulously scout for food to sustain their colony, Christians are called to actively seek out and share spiritual nourishment within their communities. This mission is crucial in a Christian's life, as it ensures that the light of Christ reaches every corner of society and strengthens the faith of others.

Matthew 5:14 says, "Ye are the light of the world. A city that is set on a hill cannot be hid." This verse highlights the Christian's role as a beacon of light in the world. Just as Pharaoh ants search tirelessly for sustenance to bring back to their colony, Christians are called to be visible examples of Christ's love and truth. Our lives should shine brightly, illuminating the path for others and guiding them towards spiritual nourishment. By living out our faith openly and authentically, we can draw others to the hope and salvation found in Jesus Christ.

Matthew 28:19 teaches, "Go ye therefore, and teach all nations, baptizing them in the name of the Father, and of the Son, and of the Holy Ghost." This verse emphasizes the Great Commission, the responsibility of every Christian to spread the gospel. Just as Pharaoh ants diligently scout for food, Christians are called to go out into the world, seeking opportunities to share the good news of Jesus Christ. This involves teaching, baptizing, and making disciples, ensuring that the message of Christ reaches all nations and peoples. By actively engaging in this mission, believers can fulfill their calling and contribute to the growth of God's kingdom.

Applying these principles to our lives means developing a mindset of seeking and sharing spiritual nourishment in various aspects of our spiritual journey. In our daily devotions, this means setting aside regular time for prayer, Bible study, and worship, making these activities a priority despite the busyness of life. Just as Pharaoh ants are consistent in their search for food, Christians should be consistent in their spiritual practices, knowing that these disciplines strengthen their relationship with God and help them grow in faith.

In our thoughts and attitudes, seeking and sharing spiritual nourishment involves setting clear priorities and avoiding distractions that hinder our spiritual growth. This means focusing on God's promises and truths rather than being swayed by worldly concerns or negative influences. By keeping our thoughts centered on God and organizing our activities around His will, we can maintain a positive and faith-filled perspective, even in challenging circumstances.

In our actions, seeking and sharing spiritual nourishment involves living out our faith with intentionality and purpose. This means making deliberate choices that honor God and reflect His character, whether in our work, relationships, or daily interactions. Just as Pharaoh ants work diligently to find and distribute food, Christians are called to act in ways that spread the gospel and serve others. By staying focused on God's mission for our lives, we can make a meaningful impact in the world and advance His kingdom.

In our relationships, seeking and sharing spiritual nourishment means being intentional about building and maintaining connections that encourage spiritual growth and mutual support. Just as Pharaoh ants communicate and work together to locate food, Christians are called to live in unity and support one another in their faith journeys. This involves being present for each other, offering encouragement and accountability, and prioritizing relationships that draw us closer to God.

In our use of time and resources, seeking and sharing spiritual nourishment involves being good stewards of what God has given us, using our time, talents, and treasures for His glory. Just as Pharaoh ants manage their resources efficiently, Christians should use their gifts and abilities to serve God and others, making the most of every opportunity to do good. This includes setting goals, managing our time wisely, and being generous with our resources.

The example of Pharaoh ants also teaches us about the importance of perseverance and resilience in seeking and sharing spiritual nourishment. Pharaoh ants do not give up when faced with obstacles but continue to work diligently until they find food. Similarly, Christians are called to persevere in their faith, even when faced with trials and difficulties. James 1:12 encourages, "Blessed is the man that endureth temptation: for when he is tried, he shall receive the crown of life, which the Lord hath promised to them that love him." By persevering in seeking and sharing spiritual nourishment, believers can grow in their faith and receive the blessings God has promised.

In addition to practical applications, seeking and sharing spiritual nourishment has deep spiritual significance. Jesus demonstrated the ultimate example of seeking and sharing spiritual nourishment during His time on earth. In John 6:35, Jesus said, "And Jesus said unto them, I am the bread of life: he that cometh to me shall never hunger; and he that believeth on me shall never thirst." Jesus was completely focused on fulfilling God's will and remained diligent in sharing the message of salvation. His single-minded dedication to His mission serves as a powerful example for Christians to follow. By developing a mindset of seeking and sharing spiritual nourishment, believers can emulate Christ's example and grow in their likeness to Him.

Seeking and sharing spiritual nourishment also play a crucial role in spiritual growth and maturity. By staying focused on God's purposes and using our gifts to serve others, Christians can avoid the distractions and temptations that hinder their spiritual growth. Hebrews 12:1-2 encourages believers to "lay aside every weight, and the sin which doth so easily beset us, and let us run with patience the race that is set before us, Looking unto Jesus the author and finisher of our faith." This verse emphasizes the importance of removing distractions and focusing on Jesus as we pursue our spiritual goals. By maintaining a mindset of seeking and sharing spiritual nourishment, believers can grow in their faith and become more effective in their service to God and others.

The principle of seeking and sharing spiritual nourishment also teaches us about the importance of integrity and consistency. Just as Pharaoh ants are consistent in their search for food, Christians are called to live with integrity and consistency in their faith. This means being the same person in private as we are in public, and living out our faith in all areas of life. By maintaining a mindset of seeking and sharing spiritual nourishment, believers can build a strong and authentic witness that draws others to Christ.

Seeking and sharing spiritual nourishment also involve setting priorities and making intentional choices. Just as Pharaoh ants prioritize their tasks for the benefit of their colony, Christians should prioritize their activities to align with God's purposes. This involves seeking God's guidance in decision-making, setting goals that reflect His will, and being intentional about how we spend our time and energy. By prioritizing God's kingdom and righteousness, believers can ensure that their efforts are focused on what truly matters.

In conclusion, Proverbs 6:6 teaches Christians to observe the Pharaoh ant and learn from its diligent and purposeful behavior. The example of Pharaoh ants scouting indoors for food sources illustrates the Christian principle of seeking out and sharing spiritual nourishment within their communities. By applying these principles to our lives, we can develop a mindset of seeking and sharing spiritual nourishment, achieve our goals, and grow in our relationship with God. Whether it is in our daily devotions, thoughts, actions, relationships, or use of time and resources, we are called to maintain a mindset of seeking and sharing spiritual nourishment. This not only brings us personal fulfillment but also glorifies God and reflects His love and wisdom to those around us. Through diligent search and sharing of God's Word, we can overcome challenges, grow stronger in our faith, and make a positive impact in the world.

Chapter 8 – Settling In Pavement - Pavement Ants

Proverbs 6:6 says, "Go to the ant, thou sluggard; consider her ways, and be wise." This verse encourages Christians to learn from the diligent and adaptable behavior of ants, which parallels the Christian principle of being adaptable and steadfast in their faith, regardless of their surroundings. Pavement ants, known for their resilience in urban environments, provide a vivid metaphor for Christians. Just as these ants thrive in the cracks and crevices of pavement, Christians are called to be adaptable and steadfast in their faith, no matter where they find themselves. This resilience and adaptability are crucial in a Christian's life, as they ensure that faith remains strong and unwavering in the face of changing circumstances and environments.

Philippians 4:11-13 says, "Not that I speak in respect of want: for I have learned, in whatsoever state I am, therewith to be content. I know both how to be abased, and I know how to abound: every where and in all things I am instructed both to be full and to be hungry, both to abound and to suffer need. I can do all things through Christ which strengtheneth me." This passage highlights the importance of contentment and adaptability. Just as pavement ants adjust to their urban surroundings and find ways to thrive, Christians are called to find contentment and strength in Christ, regardless of their circumstances. By relying on Christ's strength, believers can navigate the highs and lows of life with grace and faith.

Romans 8:28 teaches, "And we know that all things work together for good to them that love God, to them who are the called according to his purpose." This verse emphasizes the assurance that God works all things together for the good of those who love Him and are called according to His purpose. Just as pavement ants make the best of their environment, Christians can trust that God is working in all situations for their good and His glory. This trust allows believers to remain steadfast and hopeful, even when faced with challenging or unexpected circumstances.

Applying these principles to our lives means developing a mindset of adaptability and steadfastness in various aspects of our spiritual journey. In our daily devotions, this means setting aside regular time for prayer, Bible study, and worship, making these activities a priority despite the busyness of life. Just as pavement ants consistently find ways to thrive in their surroundings, Christians should consistently engage in spiritual practices that strengthen their relationship with God and help them grow in faith.

In our thoughts and attitudes, adaptability and steadfastness involve setting clear priorities and avoiding distractions that hinder our spiritual growth. This means focusing on God's promises and truths rather than being swayed by worldly concerns or negative influences. By keeping our thoughts centered on God and organizing our activities around His will, we can maintain a positive and faith-filled perspective, even in challenging circumstances.

In our actions, being adaptable and steadfast involves living out our faith with intentionality and purpose. This means making deliberate choices that honor God and reflect His character, whether in our work, relationships, or daily interactions. Just as pavement ants work diligently to establish themselves in urban environments, Christians are called to act in ways that demonstrate their faith and resilience, no matter where they are. By staying focused on God's mission for our lives, we can make a meaningful impact in the world and advance His kingdom.

In our relationships, adaptability and steadfastness mean being intentional about building and maintaining connections that encourage spiritual growth and mutual support. Just as pavement ants work together to navigate their environment, Christians are called to live in unity and support one another in their faith journeys. This involves being present for each other, offering encouragement and

accountability, and prioritizing relationships that draw us closer to God.

In our use of time and resources, adaptability and steadfastness involve being good stewards of what God has given us, using our time, talents, and treasures for His glory. Just as pavement ants manage their resources efficiently, Christians should use their gifts and abilities to serve God and others, making the most of every opportunity to do good. This includes setting goals, managing our time wisely, and being generous with our resources.

The example of pavement ants also teaches us about the importance of perseverance and resilience in maintaining faith. Pavement ants do not give up when faced with obstacles but continue to work diligently until they establish their nests. Similarly, Christians are called to persevere in their faith, even when faced with trials and difficulties. James 1:12 encourages, "Blessed is the man that endureth temptation: for when he is tried, he shall receive the crown of life, which the Lord hath promised to them that love him." By persevering in adaptability and steadfastness, believers can grow in their faith and receive the blessings God has promised.

In addition to practical applications, adaptability and steadfastness have deep spiritual significance. Jesus demonstrated the ultimate example of resilience and steadfast faith during His time on earth. In John 16:33, Jesus said, "These things I have spoken unto you, that in me ye might have peace. In the world ye shall have tribulation: but be of good cheer; I have overcome the world." Jesus was completely focused on fulfilling God's will and remained steadfast in His mission, despite facing immense challenges. His single-minded dedication to His mission serves as a powerful example for Christians to follow. By developing a mindset of adaptability and steadfast faith, believers can emulate Christ's example and grow in their likeness to Him.

Adaptability and steadfastness also play a crucial role in spiritual growth and maturity. By staying focused on God's purposes and using our gifts to serve others, Christians can avoid the distractions and temptations that hinder their spiritual growth. Hebrews 12:1-2 encourages believers to "lay aside every weight, and the sin which doth so easily beset us, and let us run with patience the race that is set before us, Looking unto Jesus the author and finisher of our faith." This verse emphasizes the importance of removing distractions and focusing on Jesus as we pursue our spiritual goals. By maintaining a mindset of adaptability and steadfastness, believers can grow in their faith and become more effective in their service to God and others.

The principle of adaptability and steadfastness also teaches us about the importance of integrity and consistency. Just as pavement ants are consistent in their efforts to thrive in urban environments, Christians are called to live with integrity and consistency in their faith. This means being the same person in private as we are in public, and living out our faith in all areas of life. By maintaining a mindset of adaptability and steadfastness, believers can build a strong and authentic witness that draws others to Christ.

Adaptability and steadfastness also involve setting priorities and making intentional choices. Just as pavement ants prioritize their tasks for the benefit of their colony, Christians should prioritize their activities to align with God's purposes. This involves seeking God's guidance in decision-making, setting goals that reflect His will, and being intentional about how we spend our time and energy. By prioritizing God's kingdom and righteousness, believers can ensure that their efforts are focused on what truly matters.

In conclusion, Proverbs 6:6 teaches Christians to observe the pavement ant and learn from its resilient and adaptable behavior. The example of pavement ants settling in urban environments illustrates the Christian principle of being adaptable and steadfast in their faith, regardless of their surroundings. By applying these principles to our lives, we can develop a mindset of adaptability and steadfastness, achieve our goals, and grow in our relationship with God. Whether it is in our daily devotions, thoughts, actions, relationships, or use of time and resources, we are called to maintain a mindset of adaptability and steadfast faith. This not only brings us personal fulfillment but also glorifies God and reflects His love and wisdom to those around us. Through resilient faith and dedication, we can overcome challenges, grow stronger in our faith, and make a positive impact in the world.

Chapter 9 – Supercolony Formation - Argentine Ants

Proverbs 6:6 says, "Go to the ant, thou sluggard; consider her ways, and be wise." This verse encourages Christians to observe the diligent and cooperative behavior of ants, which parallels the Christian principle of unity and collective effort in advancing God's kingdom. Argentine ants, known for their formation of supercolonies, provide a vivid metaphor for Christians. Just as these ants work together to form vast, interconnected colonies, Christians are called to work together in unity to further God's kingdom. This collective effort is crucial in a Christian's life, as it fosters strength, support, and growth within the faith community.

Acts 2:44 says, "And all that believed were together, and had all things common." This verse highlights the early Christian community's unity and shared resources. Just as Argentine ants form supercolonies by cooperating and sharing resources, Christians are called to live in unity, sharing their lives, resources, and support with one another. This communal living and mutual aid reflect the love and unity that Christ desires for His followers. By working together and supporting each other, believers can create a strong, unified community that advances God's kingdom and cares for its members.

Ephesians 4:16 teaches, "From whom the whole body fitly joined together and compacted by that which every joint supplieth, according to the effectual working in the measure of every part, maketh increase of the body unto the edifying of itself in love." This verse emphasizes the importance of each member's contribution to the unity and growth of the body of Christ. Just as Argentine ants each play a role in the success of their supercolony, every Christian has a unique role and contribution to make within the church. By working together and supporting one another, believers can build up the body of Christ in love, ensuring that it grows and thrives.

Applying these principles to our lives means developing a mindset of unity and collective effort in various aspects of our spiritual journey. In our daily devotions, this means setting aside regular time for prayer, Bible study, and worship, making these activities a priority despite the busyness of life. Just as Argentine ants are consistent in their cooperation and collective efforts, Christians should be consistent in their spiritual practices, knowing that these disciplines strengthen their relationship with God and help them grow in faith.

In our thoughts and attitudes, unity and collective effort involve setting clear priorities and avoiding distractions that hinder our spiritual growth. This means focusing on God's promises and truths rather than being swayed by worldly concerns or negative influences. By keeping our thoughts centered on God and organizing our activities around His will, we can maintain a positive and faith-filled perspective, even in challenging circumstances.

In our actions, unity and collective effort involve living out our faith with intentionality and purpose. This means making deliberate choices that honor God and reflect His character, whether in our work, relationships, or daily interactions. Just as Argentine ants work diligently for the good of their supercolony, Christians are called to act in ways that build up the body of Christ and serve others. By staying focused on God's mission for our lives, we can make a meaningful impact in the world and advance His kingdom.

In our relationships, unity and collective effort mean being intentional about building and maintaining connections that encourage spiritual growth and mutual support. Just as Argentine ants work together to form strong, interconnected colonies, Christians are called to live in unity and support one another in their faith journeys. This involves being present for each other, offering encouragement and accountability, and prioritizing relationships that draw us closer to God.

In our use of time and resources, unity and collective effort involve being good stewards of what God has given us, using our time, talents, and treasures for His glory. Just as Argentine ants manage their resources efficiently and share them for the benefit of the supercolony, Christians should use their gifts and abilities to serve God and others, making the most of every opportunity to do good. This includes setting goals, managing our time wisely, and being generous with our resources.

The example of Argentine ants also teaches us about the importance of perseverance and resilience in maintaining unity and collective effort. Argentine ants do not give up when faced with obstacles but continue to work diligently until their colonies are established and thriving. Similarly, Christians are called to persevere in their faith, even when faced with trials and difficulties. James 1:12 encourages, "Blessed is the man that endureth temptation: for when he is tried, he shall receive the crown of life, which the Lord hath promised to them that love him." By persevering in unity and collective effort, believers can grow in their faith and receive the blessings God has promised.

In addition to practical applications, unity and collective effort have deep spiritual significance. Jesus demonstrated the ultimate example of unity and collective effort during His time on earth. In John 17:21, Jesus prayed, "That they all may be one; as thou, Father, art in me, and I in thee, that they also may be one in us: that the world may believe that thou hast sent me." Jesus was completely focused on fulfilling God's will and desired unity among His followers. His single-minded dedication to His mission serves as a powerful example for Christians to follow. By developing a mindset of unity and collective effort, believers can emulate Christ's example and grow in their likeness to Him.

Unity and collective effort also play a crucial role in spiritual growth and maturity. By staying focused on God's purposes and using our gifts to serve others, Christians can avoid the distractions and temptations that hinder their spiritual growth. Hebrews 12:1-2 encourages believers to "lay aside every weight, and the sin which doth so easily beset us, and let us run with patience the race that is set before us, Looking unto Jesus the author and finisher of our faith." This verse emphasizes the importance of removing distractions and focusing on Jesus as we pursue our spiritual goals. By maintaining a mindset of unity and collective effort, believers can grow in their faith and become more effective in their service to God and others.

The principle of unity and collective effort also teaches us about the importance of integrity and consistency. Just as Argentine ants are consistent in their cooperation and collective efforts, Christians are called to live with integrity and consistency in their faith. This means being the same person in private as we are in public, and living out our faith in all areas of life. By maintaining a mindset of unity and collective effort, believers can build a strong and authentic witness that draws others to Christ.

Unity and collective effort also involve setting priorities and making intentional choices. Just as Argentine ants prioritize their tasks for the benefit of their supercolony, Christians should prioritize their activities to align with God's purposes. This involves seeking God's guidance in decision-making, setting goals that reflect His will, and being intentional about how we spend our time and energy. By prioritizing God's kingdom and righteousness, believers can ensure that their efforts are focused on what truly matters.

In conclusion, Proverbs 6:6 teaches Christians to observe the Argentine ant and learn from its cooperative and collective behavior. The example of Argentine ants forming supercolonies illustrates the Christian principle of unity and collective effort in advancing God's kingdom. By applying these principles to our lives, we can develop a mindset of unity and collective effort, achieve our goals, and grow in our relationship with God. Whether it is in our daily devotions, thoughts, actions, relationships, or use of time and resources, we are called to maintain a mindset of unity and collective effort. This not only brings us personal fulfillment but also glorifies God and reflects His love and wisdom to those around us. Through cooperative efforts and dedication, we can overcome challenges, grow stronger in our faith, and make a positive impact in the world.

Chapter 10 – Strong Jaws - Bulldog Ants

Proverbs 6:6 says, "Go to the ant, thou sluggard; consider her ways, and be wise." This verse encourages Christians to learn from the diligent and purposeful behavior of ants, which parallels the Christian principle of speaking truth boldly and defending their faith. Bulldog ants, known for their strong jaws, provide a vivid metaphor for Christians. Just as these ants use their powerful jaws to defend themselves and their colony, Christians are called to speak the truth boldly and defend their faith. This strength in speech and defense is crucial in a Christian's life, as it ensures that the message of the gospel is communicated effectively and that believers stand firm in their convictions.

Ephesians 4:15 says, "But speaking the truth in love, may grow up into him in all things, which is the head, even Christ." This verse highlights the importance of speaking the truth, but doing so in love. Just as bulldog ants use their strong jaws with purpose, Christians are called to use their words powerfully and lovingly. Speaking the truth in love means communicating God's Word with kindness and compassion, aiming to build others up and lead them closer to Christ. This balance of truth and love is essential for effective witness and for fostering growth within the body of Christ.

1 Peter 3:15 teaches, "But sanctify the Lord God in your hearts: and be ready always to give an answer to every man that asketh you a reason of the hope that is in you with meekness and fear." This verse emphasizes the need for Christians to be prepared to defend their faith. Just as bulldog ants are always ready to use their strong jaws to protect their colony, Christians must always be ready to explain and defend their faith with gentleness and respect. Being prepared involves knowing God's Word, understanding the reasons for our hope, and being able to communicate that hope clearly and confidently to others.

Applying these principles to our lives means developing a mindset of boldness and preparedness in various aspects of our spiritual journey. In our daily devotions, this means setting aside regular time for prayer, Bible study, and worship, making these activities a priority despite the busyness of life. Just as bulldog ants consistently use their strong jaws, Christians should consistently engage in spiritual practices that strengthen their knowledge of God's Word and their ability to communicate it effectively.

In our thoughts and attitudes, speaking truth boldly and defending our faith involves setting clear priorities and avoiding distractions that hinder our spiritual growth. This means focusing on God's promises and truths rather than being swayed by worldly concerns or negative influences. By keeping our thoughts centered on God and organizing our activities around His will, we can maintain a positive and faith-filled perspective, even in challenging circumstances.

In our actions, speaking truth boldly and defending our faith involves living out our faith with intentionality and purpose. This means making deliberate choices that honor God and reflect His character, whether in our work, relationships, or daily interactions. Just as bulldog ants use their powerful jaws to protect their colony, Christians are called to act in ways that demonstrate their faith and defend the truth of the gospel. By staying focused on God's mission for our lives, we can make a meaningful impact in the world and advance His kingdom.

In our relationships, speaking truth boldly and defending our faith mean being intentional about building and maintaining connections that encourage spiritual growth and mutual support. Just as bulldog ants work together to protect their colony, Christians are called to live in unity and support one another in their faith journeys. This involves being present for each other, offering encouragement and accountability, and prioritizing relationships that draw us closer to God.

In our use of time and resources, speaking truth boldly and defending our faith involve being good stewards of what God has given us, using our time, talents, and treasures for His glory. Just as bulldog ants manage their resources efficiently and use their strong jaws effectively, Christians should use their gifts and abilities to serve God and others, making the most of every opportunity to do good. This includes setting goals, managing our time wisely, and being generous with our resources.

The example of bulldog ants also teaches us about the importance of perseverance and resilience in maintaining boldness and preparedness. Bulldog ants do not give up when faced with obstacles but continue to use their strong jaws to protect and defend. Similarly, Christians are called to persevere in their faith, even when faced with trials and difficulties. James 1:12 encourages, "Blessed is the man that endureth temptation: for when he is tried, he shall receive the crown of life, which the Lord hath promised to them that love him." By persevering in boldness and preparedness, believers can grow in their faith and receive the blessings God has promised.

In addition to practical applications, speaking truth boldly and defending our faith have deep spiritual significance. Jesus demonstrated the ultimate example of boldness and preparedness during His time on earth. In Matthew 10:16-20, Jesus said, "Behold, I send you forth as sheep in the midst of wolves: be ye therefore wise as serpents, and harmless as doves. But beware of men: for they will deliver you up to the councils, and they will scourge you in their synagogues; And ye shall be brought before governors and kings for my sake, for a testimony against them and the Gentiles. But when they deliver you up, take no thought how or what ye shall speak: for it shall be given you in that same hour what ye shall speak. For it is not ye that speak, but the Spirit of your Father which speaketh in you." Jesus was completely focused on fulfilling God's will and remained bold and prepared in His mission, despite facing immense challenges. His single-minded dedication to His mission serves as a powerful example for Christians to follow. By developing a mindset of speaking truth boldly and defending our faith, believers can emulate Christ's example and grow in their likeness to Him.

Speaking truth boldly and defending our faith also play a crucial role in spiritual growth and maturity. By staying focused on God's purposes and using our gifts to serve others, Christians can avoid the distractions and temptations that hinder their spiritual growth. Hebrews 12:1-2 encourages believers to "lay aside every weight, and the sin which doth so easily beset us, and let us run with patience the race that is set before us, Looking unto Jesus the author and finisher of our faith." This verse emphasizes the importance of removing distractions and focusing on Jesus as we pursue our spiritual goals. By maintaining a mindset of boldness and preparedness, believers can grow in their faith and become more effective in their service to God and others.

The principle of speaking truth boldly and defending our faith also teaches us about the importance of integrity and consistency. Just as bulldog ants are consistent in their use of strong jaws, Christians are called to live with integrity and consistency in their faith. This means being the same person in private as we are in public, and living out our faith in all areas of life. By maintaining a mindset of boldness and preparedness, believers can build a strong and authentic witness that draws others to Christ.

Speaking truth boldly and defending our faith also involve setting priorities and making intentional choices. Just as bulldog ants prioritize their tasks for the benefit of their colony, Christians should prioritize their activities to align with God's purposes. This involves seeking God's guidance in decision-making, setting goals that reflect His will, and being intentional about how we spend our time and energy. By prioritizing God's kingdom and righteousness, believers can ensure that their efforts are focused on what truly matters.

In conclusion, Proverbs 6:6 teaches Christians to observe the bulldog ant and learn from its strong and purposeful behavior. The example of bulldog ants using their strong jaws to protect their colony illustrates the Christian principle of speaking truth boldly and defending their faith. By applying these principles to our lives, we can develop a mindset of boldness and preparedness, achieve our goals, and grow in our relationship with God. Whether it is in our daily devotions, thoughts, actions, relationships, or use of time and resources, we are called to maintain a mindset of boldness and preparedness. This not only brings us personal fulfillment but also glorifies God and reflects His love and wisdom to those around us. Through speaking the truth in love and defending our faith, we can overcome challenges, grow stronger in our faith, and make a positive impact in the world.

Chapter 11 – Seed Storing - Harvester Ants

Proverbs 6:6 says, "Go to the ant, thou sluggard; consider her ways, and be wise." This verse encourages Christians to learn from the diligent and purposeful behavior of ants, which parallels the Christian principle of storing God's Word in their hearts for spiritual growth and sustenance. Harvester ants, known for their practice of storing seeds for future use, provide a vivid metaphor for Christians. Just as these ants gather and store seeds to ensure they have food during times of scarcity, Christians are called to store God's Word in their hearts, ensuring they have spiritual nourishment during times of need. This practice is crucial in a Christian's life, as it ensures that believers are equipped to face challenges and grow in their faith.

Psalm 119:11 says, "Thy word have I hid in mine heart, that I might not sin against thee." This verse highlights the importance of internalizing God's Word. Just as harvester ants meticulously store seeds, Christians are called to diligently hide God's Word in their hearts. This means memorizing scripture, meditating on it, and allowing it to shape our thoughts and actions. By doing so, believers are better equipped to resist temptation and live in a way that honors God. The Word of God becomes a source of strength, guidance, and protection against sin.

Colossians 3:16 teaches, "Let the word of Christ dwell in you richly in all wisdom; teaching and admonishing one another in psalms and hymns and spiritual songs, singing with grace in your hearts to the Lord." This verse emphasizes the need for God's Word to dwell richly within us. Just as harvester ants store seeds to sustain their colony, Christians are called to let the Word of Christ dwell richly in their hearts. This involves immersing ourselves in scripture, allowing it to permeate every aspect of our lives. By doing so, we gain wisdom and are able to teach and admonish one another, building up the body of Christ. The Word of God becomes the foundation for our interactions, our worship, and our daily living.

Applying these principles to our lives means developing a mindset of diligently storing God's Word in our hearts in various aspects of our spiritual journey. In our daily devotions, this means setting aside regular time for prayer, Bible study, and worship, making these activities a priority despite the busyness of life. Just as harvester ants consistently gather and store seeds, Christians should consistently engage in spiritual practices that strengthen their relationship with God and help them grow in faith.

In our thoughts and attitudes, storing God's Word involves setting clear priorities and avoiding distractions that hinder our spiritual growth. This means focusing on God's promises and truths rather than being swayed by worldly concerns or negative influences. By keeping our thoughts centered on God and organizing our activities around

His will, we can maintain a positive and faith-filled perspective, even in challenging circumstances.

In our actions, storing God's Word involves living out our faith with intentionality and purpose. This means making deliberate choices that honor God and reflect His character, whether in our work, relationships, or daily interactions. Just as harvester ants work diligently to gather and store seeds, Christians are called to act in ways that demonstrate their faith and commitment to God's Word. By staying focused on God's mission for our lives, we can make a meaningful impact in the world and advance His kingdom.

In our relationships, storing God's Word means being intentional about building and maintaining connections that encourage spiritual growth and mutual support. Just as harvester ants work together to gather and store seeds, Christians are called to live in unity and support one another in their faith journeys. This involves being present for each other, offering encouragement and accountability, and prioritizing relationships that draw us closer to God.

In our use of time and resources, storing God's Word involves being good stewards of what God has given us, using our time, talents, and treasures for His glory. Just as harvester ants manage their resources efficiently, Christians should use their gifts and abilities to serve God and others, making the most of every opportunity to do good. This includes setting goals, managing our time wisely, and being generous with our resources.

The example of harvester ants also teaches us about the importance of perseverance and resilience in maintaining spiritual growth. Harvester ants do not give up when faced with obstacles but continue to work diligently until their storage is complete. Similarly, Christians are called to persevere in their faith, even when faced with trials and difficulties. James 1:12 encourages, "Blessed is the man that endureth temptation: for when he is tried, he shall receive the crown of life, which the Lord hath promised to them that love him." By persevering in storing God's Word in our hearts, believers can grow in their faith and receive the blessings God has promised.

In addition to practical applications, storing God's Word in our hearts has deep spiritual significance. Jesus demonstrated the ultimate example of relying on God's Word during His time on earth. In Matthew 4:4, Jesus said, "It is written, Man shall not live by bread alone, but by every word that proceedeth out of the mouth of God." Jesus was completely focused on fulfilling God's will and relied on scripture to guide and sustain Him, even in the face of temptation. His single-minded dedication to God's Word serves as a powerful example for Christians to follow. By developing a mindset of storing God's Word in our hearts, believers can emulate Christ's example and grow in their likeness to Him.

Storing God's Word in our hearts also plays a crucial role in spiritual growth and maturity. By staying focused on God's purposes and using our gifts to serve others, Christians can avoid the distractions and temptations that hinder their spiritual growth. Hebrews 12:1-2 encourages believers to "lay aside every weight, and the sin which doth so easily beset us, and let us run with patience the race that is set before us, Looking unto Jesus the author and finisher of our faith." This verse emphasizes the importance of removing distractions and focusing on Jesus as we pursue our spiritual goals. By maintaining a mindset of storing God's Word in our hearts, believers can grow in their faith and become more effective in their service to God and others.

The principle of storing God's Word in our hearts also teaches us about the importance of integrity and consistency. Just as harvester ants are consistent in their efforts to gather and store seeds, Christians are called to live with integrity and consistency in their faith. This means being the same person in private as we are in public, and living out our faith in all areas of life. By maintaining a mindset of storing God's Word in our hearts, believers can build a strong and authentic witness that draws others to Christ.

Storing God's Word in our hearts also involves setting priorities and making intentional choices. Just as harvester ants prioritize their tasks for the benefit of their colony, Christians should prioritize their activities to align with God's purposes. This involves seeking God's guidance in decision-making, setting goals that reflect His will, and being intentional about how we spend our time and energy. By prioritizing God's kingdom and righteousness, believers can ensure that their efforts are focused on what truly matters.

In conclusion, Proverbs 6:6 teaches Christians to observe the harvester ant and learn from its diligent and purposeful behavior. The example of harvester ants storing seeds for future use illustrates the Christian principle of storing God's Word in their hearts for spiritual growth and sustenance. By applying these principles to our lives, we can develop a mindset of diligently storing God's Word in our hearts, achieve our goals, and grow in our relationship with God. Whether it is in our daily devotions, thoughts, actions, relationships, or use of time and resources, we are called to maintain a mindset of storing God's Word in our hearts. This not only brings us personal fulfillment but also glorifies God and reflects His love and wisdom to those around us. Through diligent study and application of God's Word, we can overcome challenges, grow stronger in our faith, and make a positive impact in the world.

Chapter 12 – Sneaking Indoors - Ghost Ants

Proverbs 6:6 says, "Go to the ant, thou sluggard; consider her ways, and be wise." This verse encourages Christians to observe the diligent and purposeful behavior of ants, which parallels the Christian principle of being vigilant against subtle temptations and influences that can lead them astray. Ghost ants, known for their subtle and sneaky nature in infiltrating homes, provide a vivid metaphor for Christians. Just as these ants silently and subtly make their way indoors, Christians must be aware of the subtle temptations and influences that can infiltrate their hearts and minds. This vigilance is crucial in a Christian's life, as it ensures that believers remain steadfast in their faith and resist the devil's attempts to lead them astray.

1 Peter 5:8 says, "Be sober, be vigilant; because your adversary the devil, as a roaring lion, walketh about, seeking whom he may devour." This verse highlights the importance of being sober-minded and vigilant. Just as ghost ants quietly infiltrate homes, the devil uses subtle and deceptive tactics to lead Christians away from God. Being vigilant means staying alert and watchful, recognizing the signs of temptation and deceit before they can take root. Christians are called to be on guard, constantly aware of the spiritual battle they are in and the enemy's strategies. This vigilance protects their hearts and minds, keeping them aligned with God's will.

James 4:7 teaches, "Submit yourselves therefore to God. Resist the devil, and he will flee from you." This verse emphasizes the need for submission to God and resistance against the devil. Just as ghost ants can be persistent and hard to detect, the devil is persistent in his attempts to lure Christians into sin. By submitting to God and resisting the devil, believers can stand firm in their faith. Submission to God involves obedience and a willingness to follow His guidance, while resistance to the devil requires a steadfast commitment to reject sin and cling to righteousness. This dual approach ensures that Christians remain strong and protected against subtle temptations.

Applying these principles to our lives means developing a mindset of vigilance and resistance in various aspects of our spiritual journey. In our daily devotions, this means setting aside regular time for prayer, Bible study, and worship, making these activities a priority despite the busyness of life. Just as ghost ants are persistent in their infiltration, Christians should be persistent in their spiritual practices, knowing that these disciplines strengthen their relationship with God and help them grow in faith.

In our thoughts and attitudes, vigilance and resistance involve setting clear priorities and avoiding distractions that hinder our spiritual growth. This means focusing on God's promises and truths rather than being swayed by worldly concerns or negative influences. By keeping our thoughts centered on God and organizing our activities around His will, we can maintain a positive and faith-filled perspective, even in challenging circumstances.

In our actions, vigilance and resistance involve living out our faith with intentionality and purpose. This means making deliberate choices that honor God and reflect His character, whether in our work, relationships, or daily interactions. Just as ghost ants quietly go about their tasks, Christians are called to act in ways that reflect their faith, quietly but effectively resisting the influences that seek to lead them astray. By staying focused on God's mission for our lives, we can make a meaningful impact in the world and advance His kingdom.

In our relationships, vigilance and resistance mean being intentional about building and maintaining connections that encourage spiritual growth and mutual support. Just as ghost ants work together to infiltrate homes, Christians are called to live in unity and support one another in their faith journeys. This involves being present for each other, offering encouragement and accountability, and prioritizing relationships that draw us closer to God.

In our use of time and resources, vigilance and resistance involve being good stewards of what God has given us, using our time, talents, and treasures for His glory. Just as ghost ants manage to find their way into homes, Christians should be careful and intentional in how they use their resources, ensuring that their actions honor God and resist the temptations to misuse what He has provided. This includes setting goals, managing our time wisely, and being generous with our resources.

The example of ghost ants also teaches us about the importance of perseverance and resilience in maintaining vigilance and resistance. Ghost ants do not give up when faced with obstacles but continue to find ways to infiltrate. Similarly, Christians are called to persevere in their faith, even when faced with trials and difficulties. James 1:12 encourages, "Blessed is the man that endureth temptation: for when he is tried, he shall receive the crown of life, which the Lord hath promised to them that love him." By persevering in vigilance and resistance, believers can grow in their faith and receive the blessings God has promised.

In addition to practical applications, vigilance and resistance have deep spiritual significance. Jesus demonstrated the ultimate example of vigilance and resistance during His time on earth. In Matthew 26:41, Jesus said, "Watch and pray, that ye enter not into temptation: the spirit indeed is willing, but the flesh is weak." Jesus was completely focused on fulfilling God's will and remained vigilant and resistant to the devil's temptations. His single-minded dedication to His mission serves as a powerful example for Christians to follow. By developing a mindset of vigilance and resistance, believers can emulate Christ's example and grow in their likeness to Him.

Vigilance and resistance also play a crucial role in spiritual growth and maturity. By staying focused on God's purposes and using our gifts to serve others, Christians can avoid the distractions and temptations that hinder their spiritual growth. Hebrews 12:1-2 encourages believers to "lay aside every weight, and the sin which doth so easily beset us, and let us run with patience the race that is set before us, Looking unto Jesus the author and finisher of our faith." This verse emphasizes the importance of removing distractions and focusing on Jesus as we pursue our spiritual goals. By maintaining a mindset of vigilance and resistance, believers can grow in their faith and become more effective in their service to God and others.

The principle of vigilance and resistance also teaches us about the importance of integrity and consistency. Just as ghost ants are consistent in their sneaky behavior, Christians are called to live with integrity and consistency in their faith. This means being the same person in private as we are in public, and living out our faith in all areas of life. By maintaining a mindset of vigilance and resistance, believers can build a strong and authentic witness that draws others to Christ.

Vigilance and resistance also involve setting priorities and making intentional choices. Just as ghost ants prioritize their tasks for the benefit of their colony, Christians should prioritize their activities to align with God's purposes. This involves seeking God's guidance in decision-making, setting goals that reflect His will, and being intentional about how we spend our time and energy. By prioritizing God's kingdom and righteousness, believers can ensure that their efforts are focused on what truly matters.

In conclusion, Proverbs 6:6 teaches Christians to observe the ghost ant and learn from its subtle and sneaky behavior. The example of ghost ants sneaking indoors illustrates the Christian principle of being vigilant against subtle temptations and influences that can lead them astray. By applying these principles to our lives, we can develop a mindset of vigilance and resistance, achieve our goals, and grow in our relationship with God. Whether it is in our daily devotions, thoughts, actions, relationships, or use of time and resources, we are called to maintain a mindset of vigilance and resistance. This not only brings us personal fulfillment but also glorifies God and reflects His love and wisdom to those around us. Through vigilant faith and resistance to temptation, we can overcome challenges, grow stronger in our faith, and make a positive impact in the world.

Chapter 13 – Sporadic Movement - Crazy Ants

Proverbs 6:6 says, "Go to the ant, thou sluggard; consider her ways, and be wise." This verse encourages Christians to observe the diligent and purposeful behavior of ants, which parallels the Christian principle of remaining steadfast and not being easily swayed by every new doctrine. Crazy ants, known for their sporadic and unpredictable movement, provide a vivid metaphor for Christians. Just as these ants move erratically and without clear direction, there is a danger for Christians to be tossed to and fro by every new teaching if they are not grounded in their faith. This stability and steadfastness are crucial in a Christian's life, ensuring that believers are anchored in the truth and not led astray by deceptive doctrines.

Ephesians 4:14 says, "That we henceforth be no more children, tossed to and fro, and carried about with every wind of doctrine, by the sleight of men, and cunning craftiness, whereby they lie in wait to deceive." This verse highlights the importance of maturity and stability in faith. Just as crazy ants exhibit erratic behavior, Christians who are not rooted in sound doctrine can be easily swayed by false teachings. Being grounded in the truth of God's Word protects believers from being deceived and ensures that they remain on the right path. This stability allows Christians to grow in their faith and maturity, becoming more like Christ in their thoughts and actions.

1 Corinthians 15:58 teaches, "Therefore, my beloved brethren, be ye stedfast, unmoveable, always abounding in the work of the Lord, forasmuch as ye know that your labour is not in vain in the Lord." This verse emphasizes the need for steadfastness and unmovable faith. Just as crazy ants lack a steady course, Christians are called to be steadfast and unmoveable, firmly grounded in their faith and purpose. This

steadfastness enables believers to abound in the work of the Lord, knowing that their efforts are not in vain. By remaining steadfast, Christians can effectively serve God and others, making a lasting impact for His kingdom.

Applying these principles to our lives means developing a mindset of steadfastness and discernment in various aspects of our spiritual journey. In our daily devotions, this means setting aside regular time for prayer, Bible study, and worship, making these activities a priority despite the busyness of life. Just as crazy ants move unpredictably, Christians should avoid erratic spiritual practices and instead cultivate consistent and disciplined habits that strengthen their relationship with God.

In our thoughts and attitudes, remaining steadfast involves setting clear priorities and avoiding distractions that hinder our spiritual growth. This means focusing on God's promises and truths rather than being swayed by worldly concerns or new and enticing doctrines that contradict the Bible. By keeping our thoughts centered on God and organizing our activities around His will, we can maintain a positive and faith-filled perspective, even in challenging circumstances.

In our actions, being steadfast involves living out our faith with intentionality and purpose. This means making deliberate choices that honor God and reflect His character, whether in our work, relationships, or daily interactions. Just as crazy ants move sporadically, Christians are called to act in ways that demonstrate their commitment to God's truth and avoid being led astray by false teachings. By staying focused on God's mission for our lives, we can make a meaningful impact in the world and advance His kingdom.

In our relationships, remaining steadfast means being intentional about building and maintaining connections that encourage spiritual growth and mutual support. Just as crazy ants move erratically, Christians are called to live in unity and support one another in their faith journeys. This involves being present for each other, offering encouragement and accountability, and prioritizing relationships that draw us closer to God.

In our use of time and resources, being steadfast involves being good stewards of what God has given us, using our time, talents, and treasures for His glory. Just as crazy ants may scatter their efforts, Christians should use their gifts and abilities purposefully to serve God and others, making the most of every opportunity to do good. This includes setting goals, managing our time wisely, and being generous with our resources.

The example of crazy ants also teaches us about the importance of perseverance and resilience in maintaining steadfastness. Crazy ants may appear frantic and disorganized, but Christians are called to persevere in their faith, even when faced with trials and difficulties. James 1:12 encourages, "Blessed is the man that endureth temptation: for when he is tried, he shall receive the crown of life, which the Lord hath promised to them that love him." By persevering in steadfastness, believers can grow in their faith and receive the blessings God has promised.

In addition to practical applications, remaining steadfast and avoiding the sporadic movement of false doctrines has deep spiritual significance. Jesus demonstrated the ultimate example of steadfastness during His time on earth. In Matthew 7:24-25, Jesus said, "Therefore whosoever heareth these sayings of mine, and doeth them, I will liken him unto a wise man, which built his house upon a rock: And the rain descended, and the floods came, and the winds blew, and beat upon that house; and it fell not: for it was founded upon a rock." Jesus was completely focused on fulfilling God's will and remained steadfast in His mission, despite facing immense challenges. His single-minded dedication to His mission serves as a powerful example for Christians to follow. By developing a mindset of steadfastness, believers can emulate Christ's example and grow in their likeness to Him.

Remaining steadfast also plays a crucial role in spiritual growth and maturity. By staying focused on God's purposes and using our gifts to serve others, Christians can avoid the distractions and temptations that hinder their spiritual growth. Hebrews 12:1-2 encourages believers to "lay aside every weight, and the sin which doth so easily beset us, and let us run with patience the race that is set before us, Looking unto Jesus the author and finisher of our faith." This verse emphasizes the importance of removing distractions and focusing on Jesus as we pursue our spiritual goals. By maintaining a mindset of steadfastness, believers can grow in their faith and become more effective in their service to God and others.

The principle of remaining steadfast also teaches us about the importance of integrity and consistency. Just as crazy ants lack direction, Christians are called to live with integrity and consistency in their faith. This means being the same person in private as we are in public, and living out our faith in all areas of life. By maintaining a mindset of steadfastness, believers can build a strong and authentic witness that draws others to Christ.

Remaining steadfast also involves setting priorities and making intentional choices. Just as crazy ants may scatter their efforts, Christians should prioritize their activities to align with God's purposes. This involves seeking God's guidance in decision-making, setting goals that reflect His will, and being intentional about how we spend our time and energy. By prioritizing God's kingdom and righteousness, believers can ensure that their efforts are focused on what truly matters.

In conclusion, Proverbs 6:6 teaches Christians to observe the crazy ant and learn from its sporadic movement as a cautionary example. The example of crazy ants moving erratically illustrates the Christian principle of remaining steadfast and not being easily swayed by every new doctrine. By applying these principles to our lives, we can develop a mindset of steadfastness, achieve our goals, and grow in our relationship with God. Whether it is in our daily devotions, thoughts, actions, relationships, or use of time and resources, we are called to maintain a mindset of steadfastness. This not only brings us personal fulfillment but also glorifies God and reflects His love and wisdom to those around us. Through steadfast faith and a firm commitment to God's truth, we can overcome challenges, grow stronger in our faith, and make a positive impact in the world.

Chapter 14 – Soldier Heads - Big-Headed Ants

Proverbs 6:6 says, "Go to the ant, thou sluggard; consider her ways, and be wise." This verse encourages Christians to observe the diligent and purposeful behavior of ants, which parallels the Christian principle of understanding and appreciating the diversity of gifts and roles within the body of Christ. Big-headed ants, known for having distinct roles with soldier ants and worker ants, provide a vivid metaphor for Christians. Just as these ants have different functions within their colony, Christians are called to recognize and value the diverse gifts and roles within the church. This diversity is crucial in a Christian's life, as it ensures that the body of Christ functions effectively and harmoniously, with each member contributing uniquely to the mission of the church.

1 Corinthians 12:12 says, "For as the body is one, and hath many members, and all the members of that one body, being many, are one body: so also is Christ." This verse highlights the unity and diversity within the body of Christ. Just as big-headed ants have different roles but work together for the good of the colony, Christians are part of one body, each with a unique role and function. The body of Christ is made up of many members, each contributing to the overall health and mission of the church. Recognizing and embracing this diversity allows the church to operate effectively and fulfill God's purposes.

Romans 12:4-6 teaches, "For as we have many members in one body, and all members have not the same office: So we, being many, are one body in Christ, and every one members one of another. Having then gifts differing according to the grace that is given to us, whether prophecy, let us prophesy according to the proportion of faith." This passage emphasizes that each member of the body of Christ has different gifts, but all are essential and valuable. Just as big-headed ants have soldiers and workers, each performing crucial tasks, Christians are given various gifts and roles by God's grace. Using these gifts faithfully and effectively builds up the church and advances God's kingdom.

Applying these principles to our lives means developing a mindset of appreciating and utilizing the diversity of gifts within the body of Christ in various aspects of our spiritual journey. In our daily devotions, this means setting aside regular time for prayer, Bible study, and worship, making these activities a priority despite the busyness of life. Just as big-headed ants diligently perform their roles, Christians should consistently engage in spiritual practices that strengthen their relationship with God and help them grow in faith.

In our thoughts and attitudes, appreciating diversity involves setting clear priorities and avoiding distractions that hinder our spiritual growth. This means focusing on God's promises and truths rather than being swayed by worldly concerns or negative influences. By keeping our thoughts centered on God and organizing our activities around His will, we can maintain a positive and faith-filled perspective, even in challenging circumstances.

In our actions, valuing the diversity of gifts involves living out our faith with intentionality and purpose. This means making deliberate choices that honor God and reflect His character, whether in our work, relationships, or daily interactions. Just as big-headed ants work together despite their different roles, Christians are called to act in ways that demonstrate their commitment to God's mission, using their unique gifts to serve others. By staying focused on God's mission for our lives, we can make a meaningful impact in the world and advance His kingdom.

In our relationships, valuing diversity means being intentional about building and maintaining connections that encourage spiritual growth and mutual support. Just as big-headed ants work in harmony within their colony, Christians are called to live in unity and support one another in their faith journeys. This involves being present for each other, offering encouragement and accountability, and prioritizing relationships that draw us closer to God.

In our use of time and resources, appreciating the diversity of gifts involves being good stewards of what God has given us, using our time, talents, and treasures for His glory. Just as big-headed ants manage their resources efficiently and perform their roles effectively, Christians should use their gifts and abilities to serve God and others, making the most of every opportunity to do good. This includes setting goals, managing our time wisely, and being generous with our resources.

The example of big-headed ants also teaches us about the importance of perseverance and resilience in maintaining unity and utilizing diverse gifts. Big-headed ants do not give up when faced with obstacles but continue to perform their roles diligently. Similarly, Christians are called to persevere in their faith, even when faced with trials and difficulties. James 1:12 encourages, "Blessed is the man that endureth temptation: for when he is tried, he shall receive the crown of life, which the Lord hath promised to them that love him." By persevering in appreciating and utilizing the diversity of gifts, believers can grow in their faith and receive the blessings God has promised.

In addition to practical applications, valuing the diversity of gifts within the body of Christ has deep spiritual significance. Jesus demonstrated the ultimate example of recognizing and utilizing diverse gifts during His time on earth. In Ephesians 4:11-12, it says, "And he gave some, apostles; and some, prophets; and some, evangelists; and some, pastors and teachers; For the perfecting of the saints, for the work of the ministry, for the edifying of the body of Christ." Jesus equipped His followers with various gifts to build up the church and advance His mission. His dedication to equipping and empowering His followers serves as a powerful example for Christians to follow. By developing a mindset of valuing and utilizing the diversity of gifts, believers can emulate Christ's example and grow in their likeness to Him.

Valuing the diversity of gifts also plays a crucial role in spiritual growth and maturity. By staying focused on God's purposes and using our gifts to serve others, Christians can avoid the distractions and temptations that hinder their spiritual growth. Hebrews 12:1-2 encourages believers to "lay aside every weight, and the sin which doth so easily beset us, and let us run with patience the race that is set before us, Looking unto Jesus the author and finisher of our faith." This verse emphasizes the importance of removing distractions and focusing on Jesus as we pursue our spiritual goals. By maintaining a mindset of valuing the diversity of gifts, believers can grow in their faith and become more effective in their service to God and others.

The principle of valuing the diversity of gifts also teaches us about the importance of integrity and consistency. Just as big-headed ants are consistent in their roles within the colony, Christians are called to live with integrity and consistency in their faith. This means being the same person in private as we are in public, and living out our faith in all areas of life. By maintaining a mindset of valuing the diversity of gifts, believers can build a strong and authentic witness that draws others to Christ.

Valuing the diversity of gifts also involves setting priorities and making intentional choices. Just as big-headed ants prioritize their tasks for the benefit of their colony, Christians should prioritize their activities to align with God's purposes. This involves seeking God's guidance in decision-making, setting goals that reflect His will, and being intentional about how we spend our time and energy. By prioritizing God's kingdom and righteousness, believers can ensure that their efforts are focused on what truly matters.

In conclusion, Proverbs 6:6 teaches Christians to observe the big-headed ant and learn from its distinct roles and harmonious functioning within the colony. The example of big-headed ants with soldiers and workers illustrates the Christian principle of valuing the diversity of gifts and roles within the body of Christ. By applying these principles to our lives, we can develop a mindset of appreciating and utilizing the diversity of gifts, achieve our goals, and grow in our relationship with God. Whether it is in our daily devotions, thoughts, actions, relationships, or use of time and resources, we are called to maintain a mindset of valuing the diversity of gifts. This not only brings us personal fulfillment but also glorifies God and reflects His love and wisdom to those around us. Through recognizing and utilizing the diverse gifts within the body of Christ, we can overcome challenges, grow stronger in our faith, and make a positive impact in the world.

Chapter 15 – Spreading - Yellow Crazy Ants

Proverbs 6:6 says, "Go to the ant, thou sluggard; consider her ways, and be wise." This verse encourages Christians to observe the diligent and purposeful behavior of ants, which parallels the Christian principle of spreading the gospel and making disciples of all nations. Yellow crazy ants, known for their rapid and widespread movement, provide a vivid metaphor for Christians. Just as these ants quickly spread and establish themselves in new areas, Christians are called to spread the gospel rapidly and make disciples everywhere they go. This mission is crucial in a Christian's life, as it ensures that the message of Jesus Christ reaches all corners of the earth and transforms lives.

Matthew 28:19 says, "Go ye therefore, and teach all nations, baptizing them in the name of the Father, and of the Son, and of the Holy Ghost." This verse highlights the Great Commission, Jesus' command to His followers to spread the gospel and make disciples of all nations. Just as yellow crazy ants move swiftly and establish new colonies, Christians are called to go into all the world, teaching and baptizing in the name of the Father, Son, and Holy Spirit. This involves sharing the good news of Jesus Christ, leading others to faith, and helping them grow in their relationship with God. By fulfilling this command, believers participate in God's redemptive work and expand His kingdom.

Acts 1:8 teaches, "But ye shall receive power, after that the Holy Ghost is come upon you: and ye shall be witnesses unto me both in Jerusalem, and in all Judaea, and in Samaria, and unto the uttermost part of the earth." This verse emphasizes the empowerment of the Holy Spirit for the task of witnessing and spreading the gospel. Just as yellow crazy ants are known for their rapid spread, Christians are empowered by the Holy Spirit to be effective witnesses for Christ. This empowerment enables believers to share their faith boldly and effectively, reaching people in their immediate surroundings and extending to the farthest parts of the earth. The Holy Spirit provides the strength, wisdom, and guidance needed for this important mission.

Applying these principles to our lives means developing a mindset of spreading the gospel and making disciples in various aspects of our spiritual journey. In our daily devotions, this means setting aside regular time for prayer, Bible study, and worship, making these activities a priority despite the busyness of life. Just as yellow crazy ants are relentless in their spread, Christians should be relentless in their spiritual practices, knowing that these disciplines strengthen their relationship with God and prepare them for the mission of spreading the gospel.

In our thoughts and attitudes, spreading the gospel involves setting clear priorities and avoiding distractions that hinder our spiritual growth. This means focusing on God's promises and truths rather than being swayed by worldly concerns or negative influences. By keeping our thoughts centered on God and organizing our activities around His will, we can maintain a positive and faith-filled perspective, even in challenging circumstances.

In our actions, spreading the gospel involves living out our faith with intentionality and purpose. This means making deliberate choices that honor God and reflect His character, whether in our work, relationships, or daily interactions. Just as yellow crazy ants work diligently to establish new colonies, Christians are called to act in ways that demonstrate their faith and commitment to God's mission. By staying focused on God's mission for our lives, we can make a meaningful impact in the world and advance His kingdom.

In our relationships, spreading the gospel means being intentional about building and maintaining connections that encourage spiritual growth and mutual support. Just as yellow crazy ants work together to spread and establish new colonies, Christians are called to live in unity and support one another in their faith journeys. This involves being present for each other, offering encouragement and accountability, and prioritizing relationships that draw us closer to God.

In our use of time and resources, spreading the gospel involves being good stewards of what God has given us, using our time, talents, and treasures for His glory. Just as yellow crazy ants manage their resources efficiently and use them to establish new colonies, Christians should use their gifts and abilities to serve God and others, making the most of every opportunity to do good. This includes setting goals, managing our time wisely, and being generous with our resources.

The example of yellow crazy ants also teaches us about the importance of perseverance and resilience in spreading the gospel. Yellow crazy ants do not give up when faced with obstacles but continue to spread and establish themselves in new areas. Similarly, Christians are called to persevere in their faith, even when faced with trials and difficulties. James 1:12 encourages, "Blessed is the man that endureth temptation: for when he is tried, he shall receive the crown of life, which the Lord hath promised to them that love him." By persevering in spreading the gospel, believers can grow in their faith and receive the blessings God has promised.

In addition to practical applications, spreading the gospel has deep spiritual significance. Jesus demonstrated the ultimate example of spreading the gospel during His time on earth. In Luke 4:43, Jesus said, "I must preach the kingdom of God to other cities also: for therefore am I sent." Jesus was completely focused on fulfilling God's will and spreading the message of the kingdom of God. His single-minded dedication to His mission serves as a powerful example for Christians to follow. By developing a mindset of spreading the gospel, believers can emulate Christ's example and grow in their likeness to Him.

Spreading the gospel also plays a crucial role in spiritual growth and maturity. By staying focused on God's purposes and using our gifts to serve others, Christians can avoid the distractions and temptations that hinder their spiritual growth. Hebrews 12:1-2 encourages believers to "lay aside every weight, and the sin which doth so easily beset us, and let us run with patience the race that is set before us, Looking unto Jesus the author and finisher of our faith." This verse emphasizes the importance of removing distractions and focusing on Jesus as we pursue our spiritual goals. By maintaining a mindset of spreading the gospel, believers can grow in their faith and become more effective in their service to God and others.

The principle of spreading the gospel also teaches us about the importance of integrity and consistency. Just as yellow crazy ants are consistent in their efforts to spread and establish new colonies, Christians are called to live with integrity and consistency in their faith. This means being the same person in private as we are in public, and living out our faith in all areas of life. By maintaining a mindset of spreading the gospel, believers can build a strong and authentic witness that draws others to Christ.

Spreading the gospel also involves setting priorities and making intentional choices. Just as yellow crazy ants prioritize their tasks for the benefit of their colony, Christians should prioritize their activities to align with God's purposes. This involves seeking God's guidance in decision-making, setting goals that reflect His will, and being intentional about how we spend our time and energy. By prioritizing God's kingdom and righteousness, believers can ensure that their efforts are focused on what truly matters.

In conclusion, Proverbs 6:6 teaches Christians to observe the yellow crazy ant and learn from its rapid and widespread movement. The example of yellow crazy ants spreading quickly illustrates the Christian principle of spreading the gospel and making disciples of all nations. By applying these principles to our lives, we can develop a mindset of spreading the gospel, achieve our goals, and grow in our relationship with God. Whether it is in our daily devotions, thoughts, actions, relationships, or use of time and resources, we are called to maintain a mindset of spreading the gospel. This not only brings us personal fulfillment but also glorifies God and reflects His love and wisdom to those around us. Through diligent evangelism and disciple-making, we can overcome challenges, grow stronger in our faith, and make a positive impact in the world.

Chapter 16 – Snapping Jaws - Trap-Jaw Ants

Proverbs 6:6 says, "Go to the ant, thou sluggard; consider her ways, and be wise." This verse encourages Christians to observe the diligent and purposeful behavior of ants, which parallels the Christian principle of being decisive and clear in their actions and faith. Trap-jaw ants, known for their swift and decisive snapping jaws, provide a vivid metaphor for Christians. Just as these ants take quick and decisive action, Christians are called to be clear and resolute in their faith and decisions. This decisiveness is crucial in a Christian's life, as it ensures that believers are not swayed by doubts or temptations and can effectively follow God's will.

Joshua 24:15 says, "And if it seem evil unto you to serve the Lord, choose you this day whom ye will serve; whether the gods which your fathers served that were on the other side of the flood, or the gods of the Amorites, in whose land ye dwell: but as for me and my house, we will serve the Lord." This verse highlights the importance of making a clear and decisive choice to serve the Lord. Just as trap-jaw ants act swiftly with their powerful jaws, Christians are called to make firm decisions about whom they will serve. This means rejecting false idols and worldly influences and committing fully to following God. By making this clear choice, believers can ensure that their lives are aligned with God's purposes and that they are steadfast in their faith.

James 1:8 teaches, "A double minded man is unstable in all his ways." This verse emphasizes the danger of being indecisive or wavering in faith. Just as trap-jaw ants are effective because of their swift and decisive action, Christians must avoid being double-minded, which leads to instability and ineffectiveness. Being decisive in faith means having a single-minded focus on God, trusting in His promises, and acting in accordance with His will. This clarity and determination provide a solid foundation for spiritual growth and effective service.

Applying these principles to our lives means developing a mindset of decisiveness and clarity in various aspects of our spiritual journey. In our daily devotions, this means setting aside regular time for prayer, Bible study, and worship, making these activities a priority despite the busyness of life. Just as trap-jaw ants are known for their quick and decisive actions, Christians should be intentional and resolute in their spiritual practices, knowing that these disciplines strengthen their relationship with God and help them grow in faith.

In our thoughts and attitudes, being decisive involves setting clear priorities and avoiding distractions that hinder our spiritual growth. This means focusing on God's promises and truths rather than being swayed by worldly concerns or negative influences. By keeping our thoughts centered on God and organizing our activities around His will, we can maintain a positive and faith-filled perspective, even in challenging circumstances.

In our actions, being decisive involves living out our faith with intentionality and purpose. This means making deliberate choices that honor God and reflect His character, whether in our work, relationships, or daily interactions. Just as trap-jaw ants take swift and effective action, Christians are called to act in ways that demonstrate their commitment to God's mission. By staying focused on God's mission for our lives, we can make a meaningful impact in the world and advance His kingdom.

In our relationships, being decisive means being intentional about building and maintaining connections that encourage spiritual growth and mutual support. Just as trap-jaw ants work together effectively because of their decisive actions, Christians are called to live in unity and support one another in their faith journeys. This involves being present for each other, offering encouragement and accountability, and prioritizing relationships that draw us closer to God.

In our use of time and resources, being decisive involves being good stewards of what God has given us, using our time, talents, and treasures for His glory. Just as trap-jaw ants manage their resources efficiently and take swift action, Christians should use their gifts and abilities to serve God and others, making the most of every opportunity to do good. This includes setting goals, managing our time wisely, and being generous with our resources.

The example of trap-jaw ants also teaches us about the importance of perseverance and resilience in maintaining decisiveness. Trap-jaw ants do not give up when faced with obstacles but continue to act swiftly and effectively. Similarly, Christians are called to persevere in their faith, even when faced with trials and difficulties. James 1:12 encourages, "Blessed is the man that endureth temptation: for when he is tried, he shall receive the crown of life, which the Lord hath promised to them that love him." By persevering in decisiveness, believers can grow in their faith and receive the blessings God has promised.

In addition to practical applications, being decisive and clear in our actions and faith has deep spiritual significance. Jesus demonstrated the ultimate example of decisiveness during His time on earth. In Matthew 4:19-20, Jesus said to Peter and Andrew, "Follow me, and I will make you fishers of men. And they straightway left their nets, and followed him." Jesus was completely focused on fulfilling God's will and called His disciples to make a decisive choice to follow Him. His single-minded dedication to His mission serves as a powerful example for Christians to follow. By developing a mindset of decisiveness, believers can emulate Christ's example and grow in their likeness to Him.

Being decisive also plays a crucial role in spiritual growth and maturity. By staying focused on God's purposes and using our gifts to serve others, Christians can avoid the distractions and temptations that hinder their spiritual growth. Hebrews 12:1-2 encourages believers to "lay aside every weight, and the sin which doth so easily beset us, and let us run with patience the race that is set before us, Looking unto Jesus the author and finisher of our faith." This verse emphasizes the importance of removing distractions and focusing on Jesus as we pursue our spiritual goals. By maintaining a mindset of decisiveness, believers can grow in their faith and become more effective in their service to God and others.

The principle of being decisive also teaches us about the importance of integrity and consistency. Just as trap-jaw ants are consistent in their swift and effective actions, Christians are called to live with integrity and consistency in their faith. This means being the same person in private as we are in public, and living out our faith in all areas of life. By maintaining a mindset of decisiveness, believers can build a strong and authentic witness that draws others to Christ.

Being decisive also involves setting priorities and making intentional choices. Just as trap-jaw ants prioritize their tasks for the benefit of their colony, Christians should prioritize their activities to align with God's purposes. This involves seeking God's guidance in decision-making, setting goals that reflect His will, and being intentional about how we spend our time and energy. By prioritizing God's kingdom and righteousness, believers can ensure that their efforts are focused on what truly matters.

In conclusion, Proverbs 6:6 teaches Christians to observe the trap-jaw ant and learn from its swift and decisive actions. The example of trap-jaw ants snapping their jaws swiftly and decisively illustrates the Christian principle of being decisive and clear in their actions and faith. By applying these principles to our lives, we can develop a mindset of decisiveness, achieve our goals, and grow in our relationship with God. Whether it is in our daily devotions, thoughts, actions, relationships, or use of time and resources, we are called to maintain a mindset of decisiveness. This not only brings us personal fulfillment but also glorifies God and reflects His love and wisdom to those around us.

Through decisive faith and clear actions, we can overcome challenges, grow stronger in our faith, and make a positive impact in the world.

Chapter 17 – Sugar Seeking - Sugar Ants

Proverbs 6:6 says, "Go to the ant, thou sluggard; consider her ways, and be wise." This verse encourages Christians to observe the diligent and purposeful behavior of ants, which parallels the Christian principle of pursuing the sweetness of God's Word and His presence. Sugar ants, known for their attraction to sweetness, provide a vivid metaphor for Christians. Just as these ants seek out sweet substances, Christians are called to seek the sweetness of God's Word and the joy of His presence. This pursuit is crucial in a Christian's life, as it ensures that believers are continually nourished and satisfied by the truth and love of God.

Psalm 119:103 says, "How sweet are thy words unto my taste! yea, sweeter than honey to my mouth!" This verse highlights the delight and satisfaction that come from engaging with God's Word. Just as sugar ants are drawn to sweet foods, Christians should be drawn to the Word of God, finding it sweet and delightful. Engaging with scripture nourishes the soul, provides guidance, and strengthens faith. By immersing ourselves in God's Word, we can experience its sweetness and allow it to transform our lives.

Psalm 34:8 teaches, "O taste and see that the Lord is good: blessed is the man that trusteth in him." This verse emphasizes the experiential nature of God's goodness. Just as sugar ants actively seek out sweetness, Christians are invited to actively seek and experience the goodness of the Lord. Trusting in God and pursuing His presence allows us to taste and see His goodness, leading to a blessed and fulfilling life. This pursuit involves prayer, worship, and a deep relationship with God, where His presence becomes a constant source of joy and satisfaction.

Applying these principles to our lives means developing a mindset of diligently seeking the sweetness of God's Word and His presence in various aspects of our spiritual journey. In our daily devotions, this means setting aside regular time for prayer, Bible study, and worship, making these activities a priority despite the busyness of life. Just as sugar ants are relentless in their search for sweetness, Christians should be relentless in their spiritual practices, knowing that these disciplines strengthen their relationship with God and help them grow in faith.

In our thoughts and attitudes, pursuing the sweetness of God involves setting clear priorities and avoiding distractions that hinder our spiritual growth. This means focusing on God's promises and truths rather than being swayed by worldly concerns or negative influences. By keeping our thoughts centered on God and organizing our activities around His will, we can maintain a positive and faith-filled perspective, even in challenging circumstances.

In our actions, seeking the sweetness of God involves living out our faith with intentionality and purpose. This means making deliberate choices that honor God and reflect His character, whether in our work, relationships, or daily interactions. Just as sugar ants seek out and gather sweet substances, Christians are called to act in ways that demonstrate their commitment to God's Word and presence. By staying focused on God's mission for our lives, we can make a meaningful impact in the world and advance His kingdom.

In our relationships, seeking the sweetness of God means being intentional about building and maintaining connections that encourage spiritual growth and mutual support. Just as sugar ants work together to find and share sweet resources, Christians are called to live in unity and support one another in their faith journeys. This involves being present for each other, offering encouragement and accountability, and prioritizing relationships that draw us closer to God.

In our use of time and resources, pursuing the sweetness of God involves being good stewards of what God has given us, using our time, talents, and treasures for His glory. Just as sugar ants manage their resources efficiently to satisfy their need for sweetness, Christians should use their gifts and abilities to serve God and others, making the most of every opportunity to do good. This includes setting goals, managing our time wisely, and being generous with our resources.

The example of sugar ants also teaches us about the importance of perseverance and resilience in seeking God's sweetness. Sugar ants do not give up when faced with obstacles but continue to search for and gather sweet substances. Similarly, Christians are called to persevere in their faith, even when faced with trials and difficulties. James 1:12 encourages, "Blessed is the man that endureth temptation: for when he is tried, he shall receive the crown of life, which the Lord hath promised to them that love him." By persevering in seeking the sweetness of God's Word and presence, believers can grow in their faith and receive the blessings God has promised.

In addition to practical applications, pursuing the sweetness of God has deep spiritual significance. Jesus demonstrated the ultimate example of seeking the sweetness of God's presence during His time on earth. In John 15:10-11, Jesus said, "If ye keep my commandments, ye shall abide in my love; even as I have kept my Father's commandments, and abide in his love. These things have I spoken unto you, that my joy might remain in you, and that your joy might be full." Jesus was completely focused on fulfilling God's will and abiding in His love, finding joy and satisfaction in His relationship with the Father. His single-minded dedication to God's presence serves as a powerful example for Christians to follow. By developing a mindset of seeking the sweetness of God, believers can emulate Christ's example and grow in their likeness to Him.

Seeking the sweetness of God also plays a crucial role in spiritual growth and maturity. By staying focused on God's purposes and using our gifts to serve others, Christians can avoid the distractions and temptations that hinder their spiritual growth. Hebrews 12:1-2 encourages believers to "lay aside every weight, and the sin which doth so easily beset us, and let us run with patience the race that is set before us, Looking unto Jesus the author and finisher of our faith." This verse emphasizes the importance of removing distractions and focusing on Jesus as we pursue our spiritual goals. By maintaining a mindset of seeking the sweetness of God, believers can grow in their faith and become more effective in their service to God and others.

The principle of seeking the sweetness of God also teaches us about the importance of integrity and consistency. Just as sugar ants are consistent in their search for sweet substances, Christians are called to live with integrity and consistency in their faith. This means being the same person in private as we are in public, and living out our faith in all areas of life. By maintaining a mindset of seeking the sweetness of God, believers can build a strong and authentic witness that draws others to Christ.

Seeking the sweetness of God also involves setting priorities and making intentional choices. Just as sugar ants prioritize their search for sweetness, Christians should prioritize their activities to align with God's purposes. This involves seeking God's guidance in decision-making, setting goals that reflect His will, and being intentional about how we spend our time and energy. By prioritizing God's kingdom and righteousness, believers can ensure that their efforts are focused on what truly matters.

In conclusion, Proverbs 6:6 teaches Christians to observe the sugar ant and learn from its relentless pursuit of sweetness. The example of sugar ants seeking out and gathering sweet substances illustrates the Christian principle of pursuing the sweetness of God's Word and His presence. By applying these principles to our lives, we can develop a mindset of diligently seeking the sweetness of God, achieve our goals, and grow in our relationship with Him. Whether it is in our daily devotions, thoughts, actions, relationships, or use of time and resources, we are called to maintain a mindset of seeking the sweetness of God. This not only brings us personal fulfillment but also glorifies God and reflects His love and wisdom to those around us. Through a consistent and intentional pursuit of God's Word and presence, we can overcome challenges, grow stronger in our faith, and make a positive impact in the world.

Chapter 18 – Stinging Wasps - Velvet Ants

Proverbs 6:6 says, "Go to the ant, thou sluggard; consider her ways, and be wise." This verse encourages Christians to observe the diligent and purposeful behavior of ants, which parallels the Christian principle of understanding the consequences of sin and the importance of repentance. Velvet ants, which are actually stinging wasps, provide a vivid metaphor for Christians. Just as the painful sting of velvet ants serves as a warning, Christians are reminded of the painful consequences of sin and the importance of seeking repentance and forgiveness from God. This awareness is crucial in a Christian's life, as it ensures that believers remain vigilant against sin and strive to live a life pleasing to God.

Romans 6:23 says, "For the wages of sin is death; but the gift of God is eternal life through Jesus Christ our Lord." This verse highlights the severe consequences of sin, which is spiritual death. Just as the sting of a velvet ant is painful, the result of living in sin is ultimately spiritual death and separation from God. However, the verse also provides hope by reminding us that the gift of God is eternal life through Jesus Christ. This eternal life is available to all who turn away from sin and accept Jesus as their Savior. Understanding the seriousness of sin and the gift of salvation motivates Christians to live righteously and seek God's forgiveness.

1 John 1:9 teaches, "If we confess our sins, he is faithful and just to forgive us our sins, and to cleanse us from all unrighteousness." This verse emphasizes the importance of repentance and confession. Just as one would seek relief from the sting of a velvet ant, Christians are encouraged to confess their sins to God. God's faithfulness and justice ensure that He will forgive those who genuinely repent and

seek His mercy. This forgiveness not only cleanses believers from all unrighteousness but also restores their relationship with God, allowing them to live a life free from the burden of sin.

Applying these principles to our lives means developing a mindset of repentance and vigilance against sin in various aspects of our spiritual journey. In our daily devotions, this means setting aside regular time for prayer, Bible study, and worship, making these activities a priority despite the busyness of life. Just as one would avoid the painful sting of a velvet ant, Christians should be intentional about avoiding sin and seeking God's forgiveness when they fall short. Engaging in these spiritual practices helps strengthen our relationship with God and keeps us mindful of His standards.

In our thoughts and attitudes, recognizing the consequences of sin involves setting clear priorities and avoiding distractions that lead us away from God's path. This means focusing on God's promises and truths rather than being swayed by worldly temptations or negative influences. By keeping our thoughts centered on God and organizing our activities around His will, we can maintain a positive and faith-filled perspective, even in challenging circumstances.

In our actions, being mindful of the consequences of sin involves living out our faith with intentionality and purpose. This means making deliberate choices that honor God and reflect His character, whether in our work, relationships, or daily interactions. Just as one would be careful to avoid the sting of a velvet ant, Christians are called to act in ways that demonstrate their commitment to God's standards and avoid behaviors that lead to sin. By staying focused on God's mission for our lives, we can make a meaningful impact in the world and advance His kingdom.

In our relationships, recognizing the consequences of sin means being intentional about building and maintaining connections that encourage spiritual growth and mutual support. Just as one would warn others about the sting of a velvet ant, Christians are called to live in unity and support one another in their faith journeys. This involves being present for each other, offering encouragement and accountability, and prioritizing relationships that draw us closer to God.

In our use of time and resources, being mindful of the consequences of sin involves being good stewards of what God has given us, using our time, talents, and treasures for His glory. Just as one would be careful to avoid situations that lead to being stung, Christians should use their gifts and abilities to serve God and others, making the most of every opportunity to do good. This includes setting goals, managing our time wisely, and being generous with our resources.

The example of velvet ants also teaches us about the importance of perseverance and resilience in maintaining vigilance against sin. Velvet ants are known for their painful sting, but Christians are called to persevere in their faith, even when faced with the sting of sin's consequences. James 1:12 encourages, "Blessed is the man that endureth temptation: for when he is tried, he shall receive the crown of life, which the Lord hath promised to them that love him." By persevering in repentance and vigilance, believers can grow in their faith and receive the blessings God has promised.

In addition to practical applications, understanding the consequences of sin and the importance of repentance has deep spiritual significance. Jesus demonstrated the ultimate example of understanding the seriousness of sin and the necessity of repentance during His time on earth. In Mark 1:15, Jesus said, "The time is fulfilled, and the kingdom of God is at hand: repent ye, and believe the gospel." Jesus was completely focused on fulfilling God's will and called His followers to repent and believe in the good news. His single-minded dedication to God's standards serves as a powerful example for Christians to follow. By developing a mindset of repentance and vigilance against sin, believers can emulate Christ's example and grow in their likeness to Him.

Understanding the consequences of sin and the importance of repentance also play a crucial role in spiritual growth and maturity. By staying focused on God's purposes and using our gifts to serve others, Christians can avoid the distractions and temptations that hinder their spiritual growth. Hebrews 12:1-2 encourages believers to "lay aside every weight, and the sin which doth so easily beset us, and let us run with patience the race that is set before us, Looking unto Jesus the author and finisher of our faith." This verse emphasizes the importance of removing distractions and focusing on Jesus as we pursue our spiritual goals. By maintaining a mindset of repentance and vigilance, believers can grow in their faith and become more effective in their service to God and others.

The principle of understanding the consequences of sin and the importance of repentance also teaches us about the importance of integrity and consistency. Just as one would be consistent in avoiding the sting of a velvet ant, Christians are called to live with integrity and consistency in their faith. This means being the same person in private as we are in public, and living out our faith in all areas of life. By maintaining a mindset of repentance and vigilance, believers can build a strong and authentic witness that draws others to Christ.

Understanding the consequences of sin and the importance of repentance also involves setting priorities and making intentional choices. Just as one would prioritize avoiding the painful sting of a velvet ant, Christians should prioritize their activities to align with God's purposes. This involves seeking God's guidance in decision-making, setting goals that reflect His will, and being intentional about how we spend our time and energy. By prioritizing God's kingdom and righteousness, believers can ensure that their efforts are focused on what truly matters.

In conclusion, Proverbs 6:6 teaches Christians to observe the velvet ant and learn from its painful sting as a reminder of the consequences of sin and the importance of repentance. The example of velvet ants, which are actually stinging wasps, illustrates the Christian principle of understanding the seriousness of sin and the necessity of seeking God's forgiveness. By applying these principles to our lives, we can develop a mindset of repentance and vigilance against sin, achieve our goals, and grow in our relationship with God. Whether it is in our daily devotions, thoughts, actions, relationships, or use of time and resources, we are called to maintain a mindset of repentance and vigilance. This not only brings us personal fulfillment but also glorifies God and reflects His love and wisdom to those around us. Through a consistent and intentional pursuit of God's standards and forgiveness, we can overcome challenges, grow stronger in our faith, and make a positive impact in the world.

Chapter 19 – Scavenging -Rover Ants

Proverbs 6:6 says, "Go to the ant, thou sluggard; consider her ways, and be wise." This verse encourages Christians to observe the diligent and purposeful behavior of ants, which parallels the Christian principle of seeking and gathering spiritual food and resources diligently. Rover ants, known for their scavenging behavior, provide a vivid metaphor for Christians. Just as these ants diligently search for and gather food, Christians are called to seek and gather spiritual nourishment from God's Word and other spiritual resources. This diligent pursuit is crucial in a Christian's life, as it ensures that believers are continually fed and strengthened by the truth and love of God.

Proverbs 8:17 says, "I love them that love me; and those that seek me early shall find me." This verse highlights the promise that those who earnestly seek God will find Him. Just as rover ants are persistent in their scavenging, Christians should be persistent in seeking God through prayer, Bible study, and worship. Seeking God early signifies prioritizing Him in our lives and making Him the first focus of our day. By diligently seeking God, believers can experience His love, wisdom, and guidance in their lives.

Matthew 6:33 teaches, "But seek ye first the kingdom of God, and his righteousness; and all these things shall be added unto you." This verse emphasizes the importance of prioritizing God's kingdom and righteousness above all else. Just as rover ants prioritize finding food for their survival, Christians are called to seek God's kingdom and His righteousness as their primary goal. When we put God first, He promises to provide for our needs. This means living a life that reflects God's values and principles, trusting that He will take care of our material and spiritual needs.

Applying these principles to our lives means developing a mindset of diligently seeking spiritual nourishment in various aspects of our spiritual journey. In our daily devotions, this means setting aside regular time for prayer, Bible study, and worship, making these activities a priority despite the busyness of life. Just as rover ants are relentless in their search for food, Christians should be relentless in their spiritual practices, knowing that these disciplines strengthen their relationship with God and help them grow in faith.

In our thoughts and attitudes, seeking spiritual nourishment involves setting clear priorities and avoiding distractions that hinder our spiritual growth. This means focusing on God's promises and truths rather than being swayed by worldly concerns or negative influences. By keeping our thoughts centered on God and organizing our activities around His will, we can maintain a positive and faith-filled perspective, even in challenging circumstances.

In our actions, seeking spiritual nourishment involves living out our faith with intentionality and purpose. This means making deliberate choices that honor God and reflect His character, whether in our work, relationships, or daily interactions. Just as rover ants diligently search for food, Christians are called to act in ways that demonstrate their commitment to seeking and gathering spiritual resources. By staying focused on God's mission for our lives, we can make a meaningful impact in the world and advance His kingdom.

In our relationships, seeking spiritual nourishment means being intentional about building and maintaining connections that encourage spiritual growth and mutual support. Just as rover ants work together in their scavenging efforts, Christians are called to live in unity and support one another in their faith journeys. This involves being present for each other, offering encouragement and accountability, and prioritizing relationships that draw us closer to God.

In our use of time and resources, seeking spiritual nourishment involves being good stewards of what God has given us, using our time, talents, and treasures for His glory. Just as rover ants manage their resources efficiently to ensure their survival, Christians should use their gifts and abilities to serve God and others, making the most of every opportunity to do good. This includes setting goals, managing our time wisely, and being generous with our resources.

The example of rover ants also teaches us about the importance of perseverance and resilience in seeking spiritual nourishment. Rover ants do not give up when faced with obstacles but continue to search for and gather food. Similarly, Christians are called to persevere in their faith, even when faced with trials and difficulties. James 1:12 encourages, "Blessed is the man that endureth temptation: for when he is tried, he shall receive the crown of life, which the Lord hath promised to them that love him." By persevering in seeking spiritual nourishment, believers can grow in their faith and receive the blessings God has promised.

In addition to practical applications, seeking spiritual nourishment has deep spiritual significance. Jesus demonstrated the ultimate example of seeking spiritual nourishment during His time on earth. In John 4:34, Jesus said, "My meat is to do the will of him that sent me, and to finish his work." Jesus was completely focused on fulfilling God's will and found His nourishment in doing God's work. His single-minded dedication to seeking God's will serves as a powerful example for Christians to follow. By developing a mindset of seeking spiritual nourishment, believers can emulate Christ's example and grow in their likeness to Him.

Seeking spiritual nourishment also plays a crucial role in spiritual growth and maturity. By staying focused on God's purposes and using our gifts to serve others, Christians can avoid the distractions and temptations that hinder their spiritual growth. Hebrews 12:1-2 encourages believers to "lay aside every weight, and the sin which doth so easily beset us, and let us run with patience the race that is set before us, Looking unto Jesus the author and finisher of our faith." This verse emphasizes the importance of removing distractions and focusing on Jesus as we pursue our spiritual goals. By maintaining a mindset of seeking spiritual nourishment, believers can grow in their faith and become more effective in their service to God and others.

The principle of seeking spiritual nourishment also teaches us about the importance of integrity and consistency. Just as rover ants are consistent in their scavenging efforts, Christians are called to live with integrity and consistency in their faith. This means being the same person in private as we are in public, and living out our faith in all areas of life. By maintaining a mindset of seeking spiritual nourishment, believers can build a strong and authentic witness that draws others to Christ.

Seeking spiritual nourishment also involves setting priorities and making intentional choices. Just as rover ants prioritize their search for food, Christians should prioritize their activities to align with God's purposes. This involves seeking God's guidance in decision-making, setting goals that reflect His will, and being intentional about how we spend our time and energy. By prioritizing God's kingdom and righteousness, believers can ensure that their efforts are focused on what truly matters.

In conclusion, Proverbs 6:6 teaches Christians to observe the rover ant and learn from its diligent scavenging behavior. The example of rover ants searching for and gathering food illustrates the Christian principle of diligently seeking spiritual nourishment from God's Word and other spiritual resources. By applying these principles to our lives, we can develop a mindset of diligently seeking spiritual nourishment, achieve our goals, and grow in our relationship with God. Whether it is in our daily devotions, thoughts, actions, relationships, or use of time and resources, we are called to maintain a mindset of seeking spiritual nourishment. This not only brings us personal fulfillment but also glorifies God and reflects His love and wisdom to those around us. Through diligent pursuit of God's Word and presence, we can overcome challenges, grow stronger in our faith, and make a positive impact in the world.

Chapter 20 – Stealing - Thief Ants

Proverbs 6:6 says, "Go to the ant, thou sluggard; consider her ways, and be wise." This verse encourages Christians to observe the diligent and purposeful behavior of ants, which parallels the Christian principle of living honestly and avoiding dishonesty and theft. Thief ants, known for their behavior of stealing from other colonies, provide a vivid metaphor for Christians. Just as these ants take what does not belong to them, Christians are warned against dishonesty and stealing. This behavior is crucial in a Christian's life, as it ensures that believers live with integrity, honoring God's commandments and reflecting His righteousness in their actions.

Exodus 20:15 says, "Thou shalt not steal." This verse is one of the Ten Commandments and directly addresses the sin of stealing. Just as thief ants steal from other colonies, the act of stealing goes against God's law and harms both the thief and the victim. Stealing can take many forms, including taking physical items, cheating, and deceiving others for personal gain. By adhering to this commandment, Christians show respect for the property and rights of others, and they demonstrate their commitment to living a life that honors God.

Ephesians 4:28 teaches, "Let him that stole steal no more: but rather let him labour, working with his hands the thing which is good, that he may have to give to him that needeth." This verse emphasizes the importance of repentance and transformation. Just as thief ants must cease their stealing behavior to coexist harmoniously, Christians who have stolen in the past are called to stop and instead engage in honest work. Working with integrity allows Christians to provide for their own needs and to help others. This transformation from dishonesty to honest labor reflects the transformative power of God's grace and the call to live a life of integrity and generosity.

Applying these principles to our lives means developing a mindset of honesty and integrity in various aspects of our spiritual journey. In our daily devotions, this means setting aside regular time for prayer, Bible study, and worship, making these activities a priority despite the busyness of life. Just as thief ants are relentless in their pursuit of stealing, Christians should be relentless in their pursuit of honesty and integrity, knowing that these disciplines strengthen their relationship with God and help them grow in faith.

In our thoughts and attitudes, avoiding dishonesty involves setting clear priorities and avoiding distractions that lead us away from God's path. This means focusing on God's promises and truths rather than being swayed by worldly concerns or negative influences. By keeping our thoughts centered on God and organizing our activities around His will, we can maintain a positive and faith-filled perspective, even in challenging circumstances.

In our actions, avoiding dishonesty involves living out our faith with intentionality and purpose. This means making deliberate choices that honor God and reflect His character, whether in our work, relationships, or daily interactions. Just as thief ants must choose to stop stealing, Christians are called to act in ways that demonstrate their commitment to God's commandments and avoid behaviors that lead to sin. By staying focused on God's mission for our lives, we can make a meaningful impact in the world and advance His kingdom.

In our relationships, avoiding dishonesty means being intentional about building and maintaining connections that encourage spiritual growth and mutual support. Just as thief ants disrupt harmony by stealing, Christians are called to live in unity and support one another in their faith journeys. This involves being present for each other, offering encouragement and accountability, and prioritizing relationships that draw us closer to God.

In our use of time and resources, avoiding dishonesty involves being good stewards of what God has given us, using our time, talents, and treasures for His glory. Just as thief ants take what does not belong to them, Christians should use their gifts and abilities to serve God and others, making the most of every opportunity to do good. This includes setting goals, managing our time wisely, and being generous with our resources.

The example of thief ants also teaches us about the importance of perseverance and resilience in maintaining honesty. Thief ants do not give up their stealing behavior easily, but Christians are called to persevere in their faith, even when faced with the temptation to be dishonest. James 1:12 encourages, "Blessed is the man that endureth temptation: for when he is tried, he shall receive the crown of life, which the Lord hath promised to them that love him." By persevering in honesty and integrity, believers can grow in their faith and receive the blessings God has promised.

In addition to practical applications, understanding the importance of honesty and avoiding theft has deep spiritual significance. Jesus demonstrated the ultimate example of honesty and integrity during His time on earth. In Matthew 5:37, Jesus said, "But let your communication be, Yea, yea; Nay, nay: for whatsoever is more than these cometh of evil." Jesus was completely focused on fulfilling God's will and living a life of perfect integrity. His single-minded dedication to God's standards serves as a powerful example for Christians to follow. By developing a mindset of honesty and integrity, believers can emulate Christ's example and grow in their likeness to Him.

Avoiding dishonesty and theft also plays a crucial role in spiritual growth and maturity. By staying focused on God's purposes and using our gifts to serve others, Christians can avoid the distractions and temptations that hinder their spiritual growth. Hebrews 12:1-2 encourages believers to "lay aside every weight, and the sin which doth so easily beset us, and let us run with patience the race that is set before us, Looking unto Jesus the author and finisher of our faith." This verse emphasizes the importance of removing distractions and focusing on Jesus as we pursue our spiritual goals. By maintaining a mindset of honesty and integrity, believers can grow in their faith and become more effective in their service to God and others.

The principle of avoiding dishonesty and theft also teaches us about the importance of integrity and consistency. Just as thief ants must be consistent in avoiding stealing, Christians are called to live with integrity and consistency in their faith. This means being the same person in private as we are in public, and living out our faith in all areas of life. By maintaining a mindset of honesty and integrity, believers can build a strong and authentic witness that draws others to Christ.

Avoiding dishonesty and theft also involves setting priorities and making intentional choices. Just as thief ants must choose to stop stealing, Christians should prioritize their activities to align with God's purposes. This involves seeking God's guidance in decision-making, setting goals that reflect His will, and being intentional about how we spend our time and energy. By prioritizing God's kingdom and righteousness, believers can ensure that their efforts are focused on what truly matters.

In conclusion, Proverbs 6:6 teaches Christians to observe the thief ant and learn from its behavior of stealing from other colonies as a warning against dishonesty and taking what does not belong to us. The example of thief ants illustrates the Christian principle of living honestly and avoiding behaviors that lead to sin. By applying these principles to our lives, we can develop a mindset of honesty and integrity, achieve our goals, and grow in our relationship with God. Whether it is in our daily devotions, thoughts, actions, relationships, or use of time and resources, we are called to maintain a mindset of honesty and integrity. This not only brings us personal fulfillment but also glorifies God and reflects His love and wisdom to those around us. Through a consistent and intentional pursuit of God's standards and righteousness, we can overcome challenges, grow stronger in our faith, and make a positive impact in the world.

Chapter 21 – Striking Colors - Bicolored Ants

Proverbs 6:6 says, "Go to the ant, thou sluggard; consider her ways, and be wise." This verse encourages Christians to observe the diligent and purposeful behavior of ants, which parallels the Christian principle of being distinct and standing out as lights in a dark world. Bicolored ants, known for their striking colors, provide a vivid metaphor for Christians. Just as these ants stand out due to their unique appearance, Christians are called to stand out in their actions, behavior, and character. This distinctiveness is crucial in a Christian's life, as it ensures that believers reflect the light of Christ and serve as a testimony to God's transforming power in a world that often embraces darkness and sin.

Matthew 5:14 says, "Ye are the light of the world. A city that is set on a hill cannot be hid." This verse emphasizes the role of Christians as bearers of light in a dark world. Just as bicolored ants are easily noticeable due to their vibrant colors, Christians should be noticeable in their faith and actions. The light of Christ within us should shine brightly, illuminating the way for others and leading them to the truth of the gospel. By living in a way that reflects God's love and righteousness, Christians serve as beacons of hope and guidance in a world that desperately needs both.

Philippians 2:15 teaches, "That ye may be blameless and harmless, the sons of God, without rebuke, in the midst of a crooked and perverse nation, among whom ye shine as lights in the world." This verse underscores the importance of living a life that is pure and above reproach. Just as bicolored ants are distinguished by their appearance, Christians are called to be distinguished by their conduct and character. Living blamelessly and harmlessly means adhering to God's commandments, avoiding sin, and showing love and kindness to others. In doing so, Christians shine as lights in a world that is often characterized by moral and spiritual darkness.

Applying these principles to our lives means developing a mindset of distinctiveness and visibility in various aspects of our spiritual journey. In our daily devotions, this means setting aside regular time for prayer, Bible study, and worship, making these activities a priority despite the busyness of life. Just as bicolored ants are easily seen, Christians should be diligent in their spiritual practices, knowing that these disciplines help them grow in faith and shine more brightly in their daily lives.

In our thoughts and attitudes, being distinct involves setting clear priorities and avoiding distractions that hinder our spiritual growth. This means focusing on God's promises and truths rather than being swayed by worldly concerns or negative influences. By keeping our thoughts centered on God and organizing our activities around His will, we can maintain a positive and faith-filled perspective, even in challenging circumstances.

In our actions, being distinct involves living out our faith with intentionality and purpose. This means making deliberate choices that honor God and reflect His character, whether in our work, relationships, or daily interactions. Just as bicolored ants are noticeable due to their striking colors, Christians are called to act in ways that demonstrate their commitment to God's standards. By staying focused on God's mission for our lives, we can make a meaningful impact in the world and advance His kingdom.

In our relationships, being distinct means being intentional about building and maintaining connections that encourage spiritual growth and mutual support. Just as bicolored ants stand out in their environment, Christians are called to live in unity and support one another in their faith journeys. This involves being present for each other, offering encouragement and accountability, and prioritizing relationships that draw us closer to God.

In our use of time and resources, being distinct involves being good stewards of what God has given us, using our time, talents, and treasures for His glory. Just as bicolored ants manage to stand out, Christians should use their gifts and abilities to serve God and others, making the most of every opportunity to do good. This includes setting goals, managing our time wisely, and being generous with our resources.

The example of bicolored ants also teaches us about the importance of perseverance and resilience in maintaining our distinctiveness. Bicolored ants do not blend into their surroundings but remain visibly distinct, and similarly, Christians are called to persevere in their faith, even when faced with trials and difficulties. James 1:12 encourages, "Blessed is the man that endureth temptation: for when he is tried, he shall receive the crown of life, which the Lord hath promised to them that love him." By persevering in being distinct and standing out as lights, believers can grow in their faith and receive the blessings God has promised.

In addition to practical applications, being distinct and standing out as lights has deep spiritual significance. Jesus demonstrated the ultimate example of being a light in a dark world during His time on earth. In John 8:12, Jesus said, "I am the light of the world: he that followeth me shall not walk in darkness, but shall have the light of life." Jesus was completely focused on fulfilling God's will and bringing light to those in darkness. His single-minded dedication to God's mission serves as a powerful example for Christians to follow. By developing a mindset of being distinct and shining brightly, believers can emulate Christ's example and grow in their likeness to Him.

Being distinct and standing out as lights also plays a crucial role in spiritual growth and maturity. By staying focused on God's purposes and using our gifts to serve others, Christians can avoid the distractions and temptations that hinder their spiritual growth. Hebrews 12:1-2 encourages believers to "lay aside every weight, and the sin which doth so easily beset us, and let us run with patience the race that is set before us, Looking unto Jesus the author and finisher of our faith." This verse emphasizes the importance of removing distractions and focusing on Jesus as we pursue our spiritual goals. By maintaining a mindset of being distinct and standing out as lights, believers can grow in their faith and become more effective in their service to God and others.

The principle of being distinct and standing out as lights also teaches us about the importance of integrity and consistency. Just as bicolored ants are consistently noticeable due to their striking colors, Christians are called to live with integrity and consistency in their faith. This means being the same person in private as we are in public, and living out our faith in all areas of life. By maintaining a mindset of being distinct and standing out as lights, believers can build a strong and authentic witness that draws others to Christ.

Being distinct and standing out as lights also involves setting priorities and making intentional choices. Just as bicolored ants are distinguished by their appearance, Christians should prioritize their activities to align with God's purposes. This involves seeking God's guidance in decision-making, setting goals that reflect His will, and being intentional about how we spend our time and energy. By prioritizing God's kingdom and righteousness, believers can ensure that their efforts are focused on what truly matters.

In conclusion, Proverbs 6:6 teaches Christians to observe the bicolored ant and learn from its striking colors as a reminder to be distinct and stand out as lights in a dark world. The example of bicolored ants illustrates the Christian principle of living in a way that reflects the light of Christ and serves as a testimony to God's transforming power. By applying these principles to our lives, we can develop a mindset of being distinct and shining brightly, achieve our goals, and grow in our relationship with God. Whether it is in our daily devotions, thoughts, actions, relationships, or use of time and resources, we are called to maintain a mindset of being distinct and standing out as lights. This not only brings us personal fulfillment but also glorifies God and reflects His love and wisdom to those around us. Through a consistent and intentional pursuit of God's light and righteousness, we can overcome challenges, grow stronger in our faith, and make a positive impact in the world.

Chapter 22 – Soil-Dwelling - Black Garden Ants

Proverbs 6:6-8 says, "Go to the ant, thou sluggard; consider her ways, and be wise: Which having no guide, overseer, or ruler, Provideth her meat in the summer, and gathereth her food in the harvest." This verse encourages Christians to observe the diligent and purposeful behavior of ants, which parallels the Christian principle of hard work and diligence in all aspects of life. Black garden ants, known for their industrious nature in building their colonies in soil, provide a vivid metaphor for Christians. Just as these ants tirelessly work to build and maintain their colonies, Christians are called to work diligently and with purpose in their daily lives, whether in their personal spiritual growth, their work, or their service to others. This diligence is crucial in a Christian's life, as it ensures that believers are actively contributing to God's kingdom and living out their faith through their actions.

Colossians 3:23 says, "And whatsoever ye do, do it heartily, as to the Lord, and not unto men." This verse highlights the importance of working with enthusiasm and dedication, not just to please others but to honor God. Just as black garden ants work tirelessly to build their colonies, Christians should approach their tasks with the same level of dedication and commitment, recognizing that their work is ultimately for the Lord. By working heartily and with a sense of purpose, believers can bring glory to God and make a meaningful impact in the world around them.

Applying these principles to our lives means developing a mindset of hard work and diligence in various aspects of our spiritual journey. In our daily devotions, this means setting aside regular time for prayer, Bible study, and worship, making these activities a priority despite the busyness of life. Just as black garden ants are relentless in their work,

Christians should be relentless in their spiritual practices, knowing that these disciplines strengthen their relationship with God and help them grow in faith.

In our thoughts and attitudes, hard work and diligence involve setting clear priorities and avoiding distractions that hinder our spiritual growth. This means focusing on God's promises and truths rather than being swayed by worldly concerns or negative influences. By keeping our thoughts centered on God and organizing our activities around His will, we can maintain a positive and faith-filled perspective, even in challenging circumstances.

In our actions, hard work and diligence involve living out our faith with intentionality and purpose. This means making deliberate choices that honor God and reflect His character, whether in our work, relationships, or daily interactions. Just as black garden ants work diligently to build their colonies, Christians are called to act in ways that demonstrate their commitment to God's mission. By staying focused on God's mission for our lives, we can make a meaningful impact in the world and advance His kingdom.

In our relationships, hard work and diligence mean being intentional about building and maintaining connections that encourage spiritual growth and mutual support. Just as black garden ants work together to build their colonies, Christians are called to live in unity and support one another in their faith journeys. This involves being present for each other, offering encouragement and accountability, and prioritizing relationships that draw us closer to God.

In our use of time and resources, hard work and diligence involve being good stewards of what God has given us, using our time, talents, and treasures for His glory. Just as black garden ants manage their resources efficiently to ensure the success of their colonies, Christians should use their gifts and abilities to serve God and others, making the most of every opportunity to do good. This includes setting goals, managing our time wisely, and being generous with our resources.

The example of black garden ants also teaches us about the importance of perseverance and resilience in maintaining hard work and diligence. Black garden ants do not give up when faced with obstacles but continue to work tirelessly to achieve their goals. Similarly, Christians are called to persevere in their faith, even when faced with trials and difficulties. James 1:12 encourages, "Blessed is the man that endureth temptation: for when he is tried, he shall receive the crown of life, which the Lord hath promised to them that love him." By persevering in hard work and diligence, believers can grow in their faith and receive the blessings God has promised.

In addition to practical applications, hard work and diligence have deep spiritual significance. Jesus demonstrated the ultimate example of hard work and dedication during His time on earth. In John 9:4, Jesus said, "I must work the works of him that sent me, while it is day: the night cometh, when no man can work." Jesus was completely focused on fulfilling God's will and worked tirelessly to accomplish His mission. His single-minded dedication to God's work serves as a powerful example for Christians to follow. By developing a mindset of hard work and diligence, believers can emulate Christ's example and grow in their likeness to Him.

Hard work and diligence also play a crucial role in spiritual growth and maturity. By staying focused on God's purposes and using our gifts to serve others, Christians can avoid the distractions and temptations that hinder their spiritual growth. Hebrews 12:1-2 encourages believers to "lay aside every weight, and the sin which doth so easily beset us, and let us run with patience the race that is set before us, Looking unto Jesus the author and finisher of our faith." This verse emphasizes the importance of removing distractions and focusing on Jesus as we pursue our spiritual goals. By maintaining a mindset of hard work and diligence, believers can grow in their faith and become more effective in their service to God and others.

The principle of hard work and diligence also teaches us about the importance of integrity and consistency. Just as black garden ants are consistent in their work, Christians are called to live with integrity and consistency in their faith. This means being the same person in private as we are in public, and living out our faith in all areas of life. By maintaining a mindset of hard work and diligence, believers can build a strong and authentic witness that draws others to Christ.

Hard work and diligence also involve setting priorities and making intentional choices. Just as black garden ants prioritize their tasks for the benefit of their colonies, Christians should prioritize their activities to align with God's purposes. This involves seeking God's guidance in decision-making, setting goals that reflect His will, and being intentional about how we spend our time and energy. By prioritizing God's kingdom and righteousness, believers can ensure that their efforts are focused on what truly matters.

In conclusion, Proverbs 6:6-8 teaches Christians to observe the black garden ant and learn from its industrious nature in building colonies in the soil. The example of black garden ants illustrates the Christian principle of hard work and diligence in all aspects of life. By applying these principles to our lives, we can develop a mindset of hard work and diligence, achieve our goals, and grow in our relationship with God. Whether it is in our daily devotions, thoughts, actions, relationships, or use of time and resources, we are called to maintain a mindset of hard work and diligence. This not only brings us personal fulfillment but also glorifies God and reflects His love and wisdom to those around us. Through a consistent and intentional pursuit of God's work and purposes, we can overcome challenges, grow stronger in our faith, and make a positive impact in the world.

Chapter 23 – Sphere-Building - Field

Ants

Proverbs 6:6 says, "Go to the ant, thou sluggard; consider her ways, and be wise." This verse encourages Christians to observe the diligent and purposeful behavior of ants, which parallels the Christian principle of building a strong, unified community within the body of Christ. Field ants, known for their impressive sphere-shaped mounds, provide a vivid metaphor for Christians. Just as these ants work together to build and maintain their colonies, Christians are called to build a strong, unified community within the church. This unity is crucial in a Christian's life, as it ensures that believers support and strengthen one another, creating a collective witness to the world of God's love and power.

Ephesians 2:21 says, "In whom all the building fitly framed together groweth unto an holy temple in the Lord." This verse highlights the importance of unity and cohesion in the body of Christ. Just as field ants meticulously construct their mounds, ensuring each part fits perfectly together, Christians are called to be united and work together harmoniously. Each believer is a vital part of the spiritual building, and together they form a holy temple where God's presence dwells. This unity not only glorifies God but also provides a strong foundation for the church to grow and flourish.

1 Peter 2:5 teaches, "Ye also, as lively stones, are built up a spiritual house, an holy priesthood, to offer up spiritual sacrifices, acceptable to God by Jesus Christ." This verse underscores the role of each Christian as a living stone in the spiritual house of God. Just as field ants collectively contribute to the construction of their mounds, each believer contributes to the building up of the church. Christians are called to offer spiritual sacrifices through their worship, service, and daily lives. By working together in unity, they create a vibrant and effective community that reflects God's holiness and serves His purposes.

Applying these principles to our lives means developing a mindset of unity and cooperation in various aspects of our spiritual journey. In our daily devotions, this means setting aside regular time for prayer, Bible study, and worship, making these activities a priority despite the busyness of life. Just as field ants work diligently to construct their mounds, Christians should be diligent in their spiritual practices, knowing that these disciplines strengthen their relationship with God and help them grow in faith.

In our thoughts and attitudes, building a strong, unified community involves setting clear priorities and avoiding distractions that hinder our spiritual growth. This means focusing on God's promises and truths rather than being swayed by worldly concerns or negative influences. By keeping our thoughts centered on God and organizing our activities around His will, we can maintain a positive and faith-filled perspective, even in challenging circumstances.

In our actions, building a strong, unified community involves living out our faith with intentionality and purpose. This means making deliberate choices that honor God and reflect His character, whether in our work, relationships, or daily interactions. Just as field ants work together to create a cohesive structure, Christians are called to act in ways that demonstrate their commitment to God's mission and to supporting one another. By staying focused on God's mission for our lives, we can make a meaningful impact in the world and advance His kingdom.

In our relationships, building a strong, unified community means being intentional about building and maintaining connections that encourage spiritual growth and mutual support. Just as field ants rely on each other to build their mounds, Christians are called to live in unity and support one another in their faith journeys. This involves being present for each other, offering encouragement and accountability, and prioritizing relationships that draw us closer to God.

In our use of time and resources, building a strong, unified community involves being good stewards of what God has given us, using our time, talents, and treasures for His glory. Just as field ants manage their resources efficiently to ensure the success of their colonies, Christians should use their gifts and abilities to serve God and others, making the most of every opportunity to do good. This includes setting goals, managing our time wisely, and being generous with our resources.

The example of field ants also teaches us about the importance of perseverance and resilience in maintaining unity. Field ants do not give up when faced with obstacles but continue to work together to achieve their goals. Similarly, Christians are called to persevere in their faith, even when faced with trials and difficulties. James 1:12 encourages, "Blessed is the man that endureth temptation: for when he is tried, he shall receive the crown of life, which the Lord hath promised to them that love him." By persevering in unity and cooperation, believers can grow in their faith and receive the blessings God has promised.

In addition to practical applications, building a strong, unified community has deep spiritual significance. Jesus demonstrated the ultimate example of building a unified community during His time on earth. In John 17:21, Jesus prayed, "That they all may be one; as thou, Father, art in me, and I in thee, that they also may be one in us: that the world may believe that thou hast sent me." Jesus was completely focused on fulfilling God's will and prayed for the unity of His followers. His single-minded dedication to building a unified community serves as a powerful example for Christians to follow. By developing a mindset of unity and cooperation, believers can emulate Christ's example and grow in their likeness to Him.

Building a strong, unified community also plays a crucial role in spiritual growth and maturity. By staying focused on God's purposes and using our gifts to serve others, Christians can avoid the distractions and temptations that hinder their spiritual growth. Hebrews 12:1-2 encourages believers to "lay aside every weight, and the sin which doth so easily beset us, and let us run with patience the race that is set before us, Looking unto Jesus the author and finisher of our faith." This verse emphasizes the importance of removing distractions and focusing on Jesus as we pursue our spiritual goals. By maintaining a mindset of unity and cooperation, believers can grow in their faith and become more effective in their service to God and others.

The principle of building a strong, unified community also teaches us about the importance of integrity and consistency. Just as field ants are consistent in their efforts to build and maintain their mounds, Christians are called to live with integrity and consistency in their faith. This means being the same person in private as we are in public, and living out our faith in all areas of life. By maintaining a mindset of unity and cooperation, believers can build a strong and authentic witness that draws others to Christ.

Building a strong, unified community also involves setting priorities and making intentional choices. Just as field ants prioritize their tasks for the benefit of their colonies, Christians should prioritize their activities to align with God's purposes. This involves seeking God's guidance in decision-making, setting goals that reflect His will, and being intentional about how we spend our time and energy. By prioritizing God's kingdom and righteousness, believers can ensure that their efforts are focused on what truly matters.

In conclusion, Proverbs 6:6 teaches Christians to observe the field ant and learn from its sphere-building behavior as a demonstration of the value of building a strong, unified community in the body of Christ. The example of field ants illustrates the Christian principle of working together harmoniously and supporting one another to create a cohesive and effective community. By applying these principles to our lives, we can develop a mindset of unity and cooperation, achieve our goals, and grow in our relationship with God. Whether it is in our daily devotions, thoughts, actions, relationships, or use of time and resources, we are called to maintain a mindset of building a strong, unified community. This not only brings us personal fulfillment but also glorifies God and reflects His love and wisdom to those around us. Through a consistent and intentional pursuit of unity and cooperation, we can overcome challenges, grow stronger in our faith, and make a positive impact in the world.

Chapter 24 – Short Circuiting - Crazy Raspberry Ants

Proverbs 6:6 says, "Go to the ant, thou sluggard; consider her ways, and be wise." This verse encourages Christians to observe the behavior of ants, which can provide important lessons for life. Crazy Rasberry ants, known for their tendency to cause electrical short circuits, serve as a metaphor for the disruptive nature of sin in a Christian's life. Just as these ants can disrupt electrical systems, sin can disrupt a Christian's relationship with God and the smooth functioning of their spiritual life. Understanding this disruption is crucial, as it emphasizes the importance of staying vigilant against sin and maintaining a healthy spiritual walk with the Lord.

Romans 6:23 says, "For the wages of sin is death; but the gift of God is eternal life through Jesus Christ our Lord." This verse clearly outlines the severe consequences of sin. Just as the short circuits caused by Crazy Rasberry ants can lead to significant damage, sin leads to spiritual death. Sin separates us from God, bringing about death and destruction. However, the verse also provides hope by highlighting the gift of eternal life available through Jesus Christ. This gift is the solution to the problem of sin and the disruption it causes in our lives. Accepting Jesus and His sacrifice restores our relationship with God and offers us eternal life.

James 1:15 teaches, "Then when lust hath conceived, it bringeth forth sin: and sin, when it is finished, bringeth forth death." This verse explains the progression of sin from temptation to death. Just as Crazy Rasberry ants start small but can eventually cause significant damage, sin begins with a seemingly small temptation but can lead to devastating consequences. Recognizing this progression helps Christians understand the importance of resisting temptation and seeking God's help to avoid sin. By addressing sin at its inception, believers can prevent the disruption it causes and maintain a strong relationship with God.

Applying these principles to our lives means developing a mindset of vigilance and resistance against sin in various aspects of our spiritual journey. In our daily devotions, this means setting aside regular time for prayer, Bible study, and worship, making these activities a priority despite the busyness of life. Just as one would take measures to prevent Crazy Rasberry ants from causing electrical short circuits, Christians should be proactive in their spiritual practices to guard against sin. Engaging in these disciplines helps strengthen our relationship with God and keeps us mindful of His standards.

In our thoughts and attitudes, resisting sin involves setting clear priorities and avoiding distractions that lead us away from God's path. This means focusing on God's promises and truths rather than being swayed by worldly concerns or negative influences. By keeping our thoughts centered on God and organizing our activities around His will, we can maintain a positive and faith-filled perspective, even in challenging circumstances.

In our actions, resisting sin involves living out our faith with intentionality and purpose. This means making deliberate choices that honor God and reflect His character, whether in our work, relationships, or daily interactions. Just as one would avoid behaviors that could attract Crazy Rasberry ants, Christians are called to act in ways that demonstrate their commitment to God's standards and avoid behaviors that lead to sin. By staying focused on God's mission for our lives, we can make a meaningful impact in the world and advance His kingdom.

In our relationships, resisting sin means being intentional about building and maintaining connections that encourage spiritual growth and mutual support. Just as one would seek help to prevent or eliminate Crazy Rasberry ants, Christians are called to live in unity and support one another in their faith journeys. This involves being present for each other, offering encouragement and accountability, and prioritizing relationships that draw us closer to God.

In our use of time and resources, resisting sin involves being good stewards of what God has given us, using our time, talents, and treasures for His glory. Just as one would protect their electrical systems from Crazy Rasberry ants, Christians should use their gifts and abilities to serve God and others, making the most of every opportunity to do good. This includes setting goals, managing our time wisely, and being generous with our resources.

The example of Crazy Rasberry ants also teaches us about the importance of perseverance and resilience in maintaining vigilance against sin. These ants are persistent and can cause ongoing problems if not dealt with effectively. Similarly, Christians are called to persevere in their faith, even when faced with persistent temptations and challenges. James 1:12 encourages, "Blessed is the man that endureth temptation: for when he is tried, he shall receive the crown of life, which the Lord hath promised to them that love him." By persevering in resisting sin and maintaining vigilance, believers can grow in their faith and receive the blessings God has promised.

In addition to practical applications, understanding the disruptive nature of sin and the importance of resisting it has deep spiritual significance. Jesus demonstrated the ultimate example of resisting sin during His time on earth. In Matthew 4:1-11, Jesus resisted the temptations of the devil by quoting Scripture and remaining steadfast in His commitment to God's will. His single-minded dedication to righteousness serves as a powerful example for Christians to follow. By developing a mindset of vigilance and resistance against sin, believers can emulate Christ's example and grow in their likeness to Him.

Resisting sin also plays a crucial role in spiritual growth and maturity. By staying focused on God's purposes and using our gifts to serve others, Christians can avoid the distractions and temptations that hinder their spiritual growth. Hebrews 12:1-2 encourages believers to "lay aside every weight, and the sin which doth so easily beset us, and let us run with patience the race that is set before us, Looking unto Jesus the author and finisher of our faith." This verse emphasizes the importance of removing distractions and focusing on Jesus as we pursue our spiritual goals. By maintaining a mindset of vigilance and resistance against sin, believers can grow in their faith and become more effective in their service to God and others.

The principle of resisting sin also teaches us about the importance of integrity and consistency. Just as one must be consistent in preventing Crazy Rasberry ants from causing damage, Christians are called to live with integrity and consistency in their faith. This means being the same person in private as we are in public, and living out our faith in all areas of life. By maintaining a mindset of vigilance and resistance against sin, believers can build a strong and authentic witness that draws others to Christ.

Resisting sin also involves setting priorities and making intentional choices. Just as one would prioritize actions to protect against Crazy Rasberry ants, Christians should prioritize their activities to align with God's purposes. This involves seeking God's guidance in decision-making, setting goals that reflect His will, and being intentional about how we spend our time and energy. By prioritizing God's kingdom and righteousness, believers can ensure that their efforts are focused on what truly matters.

In conclusion, Proverbs 6:6 teaches Christians to observe the Crazy Rasberry ant and learn from its disruptive behavior as a metaphor for the nature of sin in a Christian's life. The example of these ants causing electrical short circuits illustrates the Christian principle of understanding the severity of sin and the importance of resisting it. By applying these principles to our lives, we can develop a mindset of vigilance and resistance against sin, achieve our goals, and grow in our relationship with God. Whether it is in our daily devotions, thoughts, actions, relationships, or use of time and resources, we are called to maintain a mindset of vigilance and resistance against sin. This not only brings us personal fulfillment but also glorifies God and reflects His love and wisdom to those around us. Through a consistent and intentional pursuit of God's righteousness and vigilance against sin, we can overcome challenges, grow stronger in our faith, and make a positive impact in the world.

Chapter 25 – Stealthy Nesting - Ghost Ants

Proverbs 6:6 says, "Go to the ant, thou sluggard; consider her ways, and be wise." This verse encourages Christians to observe the behavior of ants, which can provide important lessons for life. Ghost ants, known for their stealthy nesting habits, serve as a metaphor for the subtle spiritual dangers that Christians must be aware of. Just as these ants can build nests unnoticed, spiritual dangers can infiltrate a Christian's life quietly and gradually, causing significant harm if not addressed. Recognizing and staying vigilant against these dangers is crucial, as it helps Christians maintain a healthy spiritual walk with the Lord.

1 Peter 5:8 says, "Be sober, be vigilant; because your adversary the devil, as a roaring lion, walketh about, seeking whom he may devour." This verse highlights the importance of vigilance in the Christian life. Just as ghost ants are stealthy and can establish nests without being detected, the devil seeks to attack believers in subtle and deceptive ways. Christians are called to be sober and vigilant, always on guard against spiritual threats. This vigilance involves staying alert to the influences and temptations that can lead us away from God and being proactive in our faith to resist them.

Ephesians 6:11 teaches, "Put on the whole armour of God, that ye may be able to stand against the wiles of the devil." This verse emphasizes the need for spiritual preparedness. Just as one would take measures to prevent ghost ants from nesting in their home, Christians are called to equip themselves with the whole armor of God to stand against the devil's schemes. This armor includes truth, righteousness, the gospel of peace, faith, salvation, the Word of God, and prayer. By putting on this armor, believers can defend themselves against spiritual dangers and remain steadfast in their faith.

Applying these principles to our lives means developing a mindset of vigilance and spiritual preparedness in various aspects of our spiritual journey. In our daily devotions, this means setting aside regular time for prayer, Bible study, and worship, making these activities a priority despite the busyness of life. Just as one would be diligent in preventing ghost ants from nesting unnoticed, Christians should be diligent in their spiritual practices to guard against subtle spiritual dangers. Engaging in these disciplines helps strengthen our relationship with God and keeps us mindful of His standards.

In our thoughts and attitudes, vigilance involves setting clear priorities and avoiding distractions that lead us away from God's path. This means focusing on God's promises and truths rather than being swayed by worldly concerns or negative influences. By keeping our thoughts centered on God and organizing our activities around His will, we can maintain a positive and faith-filled perspective, even in challenging circumstances.

In our actions, vigilance involves living out our faith with intentionality and purpose. This means making deliberate choices that honor God and reflect His character, whether in our work, relationships, or daily interactions. Just as one would take steps to prevent ghost ants from establishing nests, Christians are called to act in ways that demonstrate their commitment to God's standards and avoid behaviors that lead to spiritual danger. By staying focused on

God's mission for our lives, we can make a meaningful impact in the world and advance His kingdom.

In our relationships, vigilance means being intentional about building and maintaining connections that encourage spiritual growth and mutual support. Just as one would seek help to prevent or eliminate ghost ants, Christians are called to live in unity and support one another in their faith journeys. This involves being present for each other, offering encouragement and accountability, and prioritizing relationships that draw us closer to God.

In our use of time and resources, vigilance involves being good stewards of what God has given us, using our time, talents, and treasures for His glory. Just as one would protect their home from ghost ants, Christians should use their gifts and abilities to serve God and others, making the most of every opportunity to do good. This includes setting goals, managing our time wisely, and being generous with our resources.

The example of ghost ants also teaches us about the importance of perseverance and resilience in maintaining vigilance. Ghost ants are persistent and can cause ongoing problems if not dealt with effectively. Similarly, Christians are called to persevere in their faith, even when faced with persistent temptations and challenges. James 1:12 encourages, "Blessed is the man that endureth temptation: for when he is tried, he shall receive the crown of life, which the Lord hath promised to them that love him." By persevering in vigilance and maintaining a strong faith, believers can grow in their faith and receive the blessings God has promised.

In addition to practical applications, understanding the importance of vigilance against subtle spiritual dangers has deep spiritual significance. Jesus demonstrated the ultimate example of vigilance during His time on earth. In Matthew 26:41, Jesus said to His disciples, "Watch and pray, that ye enter not into temptation: the spirit indeed is willing, but the flesh is weak." Jesus was completely focused on fulfilling God's will and remained vigilant in His prayers and actions. His single-minded dedication to vigilance serves as a powerful example for Christians to follow. By developing a mindset of vigilance and spiritual preparedness, believers can emulate Christ's example and grow in their likeness to Him.

Vigilance against subtle spiritual dangers also plays a crucial role in spiritual growth and maturity. By staying focused on God's purposes and using our gifts to serve others, Christians can avoid the distractions and temptations that hinder their spiritual growth. Hebrews 12:1-2 encourages believers to "lay aside every weight, and the sin which doth so easily beset us, and let us run with patience the race that is set before us, Looking unto Jesus the author and finisher of our faith." This verse emphasizes the importance of removing distractions and focusing on Jesus as we pursue our spiritual goals. By maintaining a mindset of vigilance and spiritual preparedness, believers can grow in their faith and become more effective in their service to God and others.

The principle of vigilance also teaches us about the importance of integrity and consistency. Just as one must be consistent in preventing ghost ants from causing damage, Christians are called to live with integrity and consistency in their faith. This means being the same person in private as we are in public, and living out our faith in all areas of life. By maintaining a mindset of vigilance and spiritual preparedness, believers can build a strong and authentic witness that draws others to Christ.

Vigilance also involves setting priorities and making intentional choices. Just as one would prioritize actions to protect against ghost ants, Christians should prioritize their activities to align with God's purposes. This involves seeking God's guidance in decision-making, setting goals that reflect His will, and being intentional about how we spend our time and energy. By prioritizing God's kingdom and righteousness, believers can ensure that their efforts are focused on what truly matters.

In conclusion, Proverbs 6:6 teaches Christians to observe the ghost ant and learn from its stealthy nesting habits as a metaphor for the subtle spiritual dangers in a Christian's life. The example of these ants highlights the Christian principle of staying vigilant and aware of potential spiritual threats. By applying these principles to our lives, we can develop a mindset of vigilance and spiritual preparedness, achieve our goals, and grow in our relationship with God. Whether it is in our daily devotions, thoughts, actions, relationships, or use of time and resources, we are called to maintain a mindset of vigilance and spiritual preparedness. This not only brings us personal fulfillment but also glorifies God and reflects His love and wisdom to those around us. Through a consistent and intentional pursuit of God's righteousness and vigilance against subtle spiritual dangers, we can overcome challenges, grow stronger in our faith, and make a positive impact in the world.

Conclusion

As we conclude "Consider The Ant - God's Tiny Preachers," it is clear that these small creatures, often overlooked and underestimated, hold within their intricate lives the essence of spiritual wisdom that can transform our Christian journey. From the tireless worker ant to the courageous soldier, and from the purposeful queen to the unified colony, each type of ant serves as a powerful metaphor for the Christian life, offering us deep insights into how we can live out our faith in a way that pleases God and benefits the body of Christ. The worker ant's relentless dedication reminds us that our service in God's kingdom, no matter how small or unnoticed, is vital and precious in His sight. The soldier ant's unwavering commitment to defending the colony challenges us to stand firm in the spiritual battles we face, armed with the truth of God's Word and the power of prayer. The queen ant, with her unique role of nurturing and leading, calls us to embrace the purpose and leadership God has entrusted to us, fulfilling our divine assignments with humility and grace. And finally, the harmonious community within the ant colony mirrors the unity and cooperation that should characterize the local church, where each member, with their unique gifts, works together to advance God's kingdom on earth. Through the lens of these tiny preachers, we have seen that the principles of diligence, perseverance, leadership, and unity are not just lofty ideals but practical realities that can and should be lived out in our daily walk with God. As we leave this exploration of the ant's world, may we be inspired to carry these lessons into our own lives, letting the wisdom of these small creatures guide us in our pursuit of a deeper, more authentic relationship with Christ. Let us remember that in God's grand design, even the smallest of His creations has something to teach us, and as we heed these lessons, we become more fully equipped to live out our calling as His faithful servants. May the wisdom of the ant not only enrich our understanding but also transform our lives, leading us to greater diligence in our work, deeper commitment in our spiritual battles, more purposeful leadership in our local churches, and a stronger unity within the body of Christ. In doing so, we will truly reflect the glory of God's kingdom, just as these tiny preachers reflect the intricate and purposeful design of their Creator.

Don't miss out!

Visit the website below and you can sign up to receive emails whenever Joshua Rhoades publishes a new book. There's no charge and no obligation.

https://books2read.com/r/B-A-AJLBB-LPQUE

BOOKS 2 READ

Connecting independent readers to independent writers.

Did you love *Consider The Ant - God's Tiny Preachers*? Then you should read *HOOK, LINE & SAVIOUR - Faith Reflections from Fishing*[1] by Joshua Rhoades!

"Hook, Line, and Saviour: Faith Reflections from Fishing" is an engaging book for both the young and not so young, blending fishing with Christian faith principles. Through 24 chapters, it draws parallels between fishing techniques and the Christian life, making spiritual lessons relatable and fun.It starts with "Chapter 1 - Research and Knowledge," emphasizing the importance of understanding and preparation in both fishing and faith. "Chapter 2 - Choosing the Right Gear" draws a parallel between selecting the right fishing tools and using spiritual tools like prayer and scripture."Chapter 3 - Learning to Cast" highlights the need for skill and practice, comparing it to sharing

---

1. https://books2read.com/u/brjDGE

2. https://books2read.com/u/brjDGE

one's faith. "Chapter 4 - Understanding Weather Conditions" connects the importance of weather awareness for fishing to understanding spiritual and emotional climates. "Chapter 5 - Tide and Water Currents" uses tides to illustrate how life's changes can be navigated with trust in God.In "Chapter 6 - Selecting the Right Bait," using the right bait attracts fish, just as kindness and love draw others to faith. "Chapter 7 - Tackle Box Organization" underscores being spiritually organized and prepared. "Chapter 8 - Knot Tying" emphasizes building strong relationships with God and others, like tying secure knots."Chapter 9 - Boat Maintenance" compares maintaining faith through prayer to keeping a boat in good condition. "Chapter 10 - Fishing Regulations" highlights adhering to God's commandments, like following fishing laws. "Chapter 11 - Fish Finder Technology" parallels using technology to locate fish with seeking guidance through prayer."Chapter 12 - Patience and Persistence" teaches that both fishing and faith require waiting and perseverance. "Chapter 13 - Observation Skills" encourages attentiveness to God's work, like a fisherman watches for fish. "Chapter 14 - Casting Techniques" and "Chapter 15 - Reeling Techniques" relate fishing skills to guiding others to faith."Chapter 16 - Fishing Ethics" emphasizes integrity and honesty in fishing and life. "Chapter 17 - Adapting to Seasons" discusses embracing God's plan through life's phases. "Chapter 18 - Using Scents and Attractants" highlights living a life that draws others to Christ."Chapter 19 - Fishing Logs" suggests keeping a faith journal to track growth. "Chapter 20 - Joining a Fishing Community" underscores fellowship and support. "Chapter 21 - Safety Precautions" parallels physical safety measures in fishing with spiritual protection."Chapter 22 - Learning from Experts" encourages seeking wisdom from mentors. "Chapter 23 - Adapting to Different Waters" relates to being adaptable in life. "Chapter 24 - Staying Informed" emphasizes continuous spiritual growth.Overall, "Hook, Line, and Saviour" makes learning about faith accessible and enjoyable. Through practical application it encourages spiritual growth and helps readers apply Christian principles in daily life. This book is an adventurous guide that deepens faith through the exciting world of fishing, making spiritual growth enriching and fun.

www.ingramcontent.com/pod-product-compliance
Lightning Source LLC
Chambersburg PA
CBHW022016150726

47990CB00002B/684